Season's Greetings

CHRISTMAS LETTERS
FROM THOSE
WHO WERE THERE

RUTH L. BOLING

UPPER
ROOM BOOKS®
NASHVILLE

ISBN: 978-0-8358-2044-8
Epub ISBN: 978-0-8358-2045-5

Cover design: Spencer Fuller, Faceout Studio
Interior design: PerfecType, Nashville, TN

Printed in the United States of America

This book is dedicated to my nieces and nephews . . .

Diana
Fausto
Patricia
Amani
Emily
David
Laura
Michael
Megan
Andrew
Erin
George
Carolyn
Peter
Sarah
Alejandra
Anita

. . . and to their beloveds, present and future.

Chapter 5 is dedicated to my son, Daniel.

CONTENTS

Introduction   7

1 The End of Me   13
       A Letter from King Herod

2 Beyond Me   21
       A Letter from Elizabeth

3 Standing and Pointing   31
       A Letter from John the Baptist

4 Being Quiet for a Change   41
       A Letter from Zechariah

5 A Summons   53
       A Letter from Isaiah of Jerusalem

6 What God Brings   63
       A Letter from the Innkeeper

7 No Holiday   71
       A Letter from the Midwife

8 Nobody Important   81
       A Letter from a Shepherd

CONTENTS

9 Christmas Casualties   89
   A Letter from Joseph

10 Bring It   99
   A Letter from Mary

11 Gobsmacked   111
   A Letter from the Wise Men

12 One Divine Detail   121
   A Letter from Jesus

13 A Letter from You   131

A Note for Clergy and Church Leaders   135

Suggestions for Small-Group Study   139

Acknowledgments   143

INTRODUCTION

Ask a roomful of people to finish the sentence, "It's not Christmas if . . . ," and you'll get a room full of answers. It's not Christmas if it doesn't snow. It's not Christmas without matching pajamas. It's not Christmas until we place baby Jesus in the manger on Christmas morning. It's not Christmas without a sprinkling of nutmeg on the eggnog. And so on.

Underneath the hype, the traditions, and nostalgia of Christmas rests its deeper spiritual and authentically human significance. Christmas has become big, huge deal in our culture because it is, in fact, a big, huge deal! It's so huge and so full of meaning, that language fails and emotions kick in. We all want to have a "good" Christmas, and we all want the children we know and love to have a "good" Christmas, but we are hard-pressed to put into words exactly what we mean by that. When it comes to Christmas, we are not rational creatures. Unclear and conflicting expectations can be a recipe for disappointment.

I know fully grown adults who love Christmas so much they start their Christmas countdown in the middle of summer. They're the ones who watch the same sentimental Christmas movies every year with Kleenex at hand, dabbing their eyes at the exact same scenes as before. But I also know people who feel steadily worse as the holidays approach. They soldier their way through the days of December determined to hide their loneliness and push grief aside. They grit their teeth and keep their head down to avoid the sniping between family members.

I know people who think Christmas should be a simple affair, the simpler the better, and I know people who feel that anything less than a mountain of presents is unacceptable and a table laden with more food than anyone could possibly eat is the only right way to celebrate. I know people who are so thoroughly fed up with the commercialized Christmas juggernaut that they won't step foot in a big box store until the season is over and the decorations are put away for another year, and I know people who drive around all year long with "Jesus is the Reason for the Season" bumper stickers on their car.

I know parents who spare no effort devising ingenious ways to shore up their children's belief in Santa Claus (for just one more year), but leave the birth of Jesus to speak for itself. I know pillars of the church who joyfully visit nursing homes and pray with the elderly during the week, then dress up as Santa on weekends with equal enthusiasm. I know people who flat out don't believe that God came to earth in Jesus Christ, and people who could not possibly miss singing "Silent Night" at the end of a candlelight service on Christmas Eve. Sometimes they are one and the same!

Let me add that I don't just know *of* these people, I *know* them. I *love* them. They are members of the congregations I've served. They are my high school and college friends, my nieces and nephews, my colleagues, my critics, and my champions.

You know them, too.

Over the course of my three decades in ordained ministry, I've witnessed more people leaving churches than joining them. However, I know for a fact that those who leave church do not abandon their spiritual journeys, and those who stay do not stop asking thoughtful questions.

This book is for all of them. It's for the leavers and the joiners. It's for the spiritually curious and the unapologetically devout. It's for the ones who know their Bibles inside out and the ones who don't know Corinthians from Chronicles.

Clichés about the *true* "meaning of Christmas" abound but clichés are the spiritual equivalent of junk food. Their empty calories provide an immediate boost, a brief sugar high, but deliver none of the nutrients necessary for healthy living. Like junk food, Christmas clichés leave us wanting. They appeal to us in the moment but fail to satiate our hunger for something authentic, holy, and true.

Eons ago, something world-changing and life-giving happened in the little town of Bethlehem. Something holy. Something revolutionary. Something that defied logic by transcending it. This paradigm-shattering something is both a mirror into our own souls and a window into the sacred center of all that we are and of all that is. We would be fools to ignore it.

This book attempts to put that ineffable something into words. It resists the notion that there is one true meaning of Christmas. Instead, it offers multiple interpretations from a dozen different viewpoints so as to navigate a theological conversation that transcends time, culture, and geography.

I was raised the daughter of a biblical scholar. That means I approach biblical studies with fear and trembling. I do my research and I work hard to separate my preconceived ideas from what is actually stated in the biblical texts. I am also a writer, a pastor, an educator, a middle-class white American, a wife, a mother, and a feminist—that is to say, a veritable hodgepodge of twenty-first century identities. As much as the letters in this book originate from the holy scriptures, so also do they emerge from me. I believe this is by God's grace and by God's design.

I don't believe there is any such thing as an objective study of scripture. The scriptures are God's Word to human beings, not *theoretical* human beings but *actual* human beings who live and breathe and learn in particular communities under particular circumstances. This book is one human being's attempt at putting the truth—or rather, the truths—of Christmas into words. I hope it will help you do likewise.

Each chapter takes the form of a letter written to twenty-first century readers by one of the biblical characters involved in the Christmas story. Some are well-known and some are less so. Each letter tackles the subject, "What Christmas Means to Me," from a different perspective. The letters are grounded in the biblical texts referred to at the beginning of each chapter, to which I have added details, scenes, and plot points that I believe are in keeping with the deeper truths of the narrative. I leave it to you to sort out what does and does not ring true for you.

Getting Ready

There is no right or wrong way to read this book, but here are a few ideas to put things in context and help you get started.

First, take a few moments to set the stage. If you own a nativity set, dig it out of your closet and set it up as a focal point in your home. Alternatively, you might arrange a display of Christmas cards that portray scenes from Christ's birth or hang nativity-themed ornaments front and center on your Christmas tree.

Study the nativity characters as they are portrayed. What style did the artist or craftsman select? What details are included? What facial expressions are conveyed? What feelings are evoked? Try to imagine each character as a living, breathing ordinary human being taking part in the events of Christmas. Ask each character, "What did you know about the significance of your part in the story, and when did you know it?"

Next, look over the chapter headings in this book. Notice which characters from your nativity scene match up with the various chapters. Who is there? Who is missing? Imagine expanding the figures in your nativity scene to include a wider cast of characters. You may even want to add common household objects to serve as stand-ins for the missing characters or write their names on sticky notes or index cards. What thoughts, questions, or feelings do these additional characters elicit?

Each chapter includes journaling prompts for reflection and spiritual growth, so keep a journal or a notebook handy while you read. At the end of the book, I'll invite you to write your own letter addressing the subject, "What Christmas Means to Me," so consider jotting down notes as you go.

Some of you may choose to read this book with a friend, family member, or group. Others may prefer a solo read. Each chapter includes scripture references, prayers, and questions for reflection with every sort of reader in mind.

Last, but not least, permission is hereby given for clergy and church leaders to use or adapt the letters in each chapter as sermons, with attribution. See the "Afterword for Clergy and Church Leaders" for more ideas on using this book with your congregation.

CHAPTER ONE

The End of Me
A Letter from King Herod

Matthew 2:1-18

TO WHOM IT MAY CONCERN:

I am Herod the Great. Or, I *was* Herod the Great.

The question of what Christmas means to me is a sore subject. I don't want to write about it. Christmas ruined me. It tarnished my reputation. It destroyed my legacy. In the great drama of human history, that penniless child born in that ridiculous stable in Bethlehem upstaged me. Me—Herod the Great. Christmas was the worst thing that ever happened to me. I tried to eradicate it. I should have tried harder.

If you want to know what Christmas means to me, let's start with the word *me*. Let me tell you about me. If it weren't for Jesus grabbing all the oxygen in the room for the last 2,000 years, you would know a lot more about me. I am called "Herod the Great" for good reason.

My father was an Edomite, you would call him an Arab today, and he lived in what is now known as southern Jordan. My mother came from a noble Nabatean family from the great city of Petra. Our people converted to Judaism a hundred years or so before I was born. When the Romans invaded Palestine in 63 CE, my father, Antipar, sided with Rome. For that, our Jewish family was granted Roman citizenship and rewarded with power. I made friends with Mark Antony, of *Antony and Cleopatra* fame, and I leveraged that friendship throughout my shining career. When I was just twenty-five years old, the Romans appointed me to be the provincial governor of Galilee. At age thirty-six, I was named by the Roman senate as king of Judea; that is, "king of the Jews." Let that sink in for a minute.

I was a Jew. I was a Roman citizen. *I* was king of the Jews.

One of my greatest accomplishments was to completely rebuild *and* expand the Temple in Jerusalem. King Solomon gets pages and pages of credit in the Bible for building the Temple, but his Temple got destroyed. I rebuilt it. Magnificently! In keeping with Jewish law, I employed 1,000 priests as masons and carpenters. But do I get any credit for that in the Bible? No, I do not. Do any of you know any Bible verses extolling my virtue in restoring the Temple? No, you don't. Because there aren't any. That's just one of the many reasons Christmas enrages me. If it weren't for him, for that baby, Jesus, I would be remembered as a Bible hero. Instead, I'm a Bible villain.

If you take a trip to the Holy Land today, the tour buses will stop and show you what remains of all my magnificent building projects. You will see Masada, a clifftop palace-fortress decorated with intricate mosaics and equipped with water cisterns to withstand a lengthy siege. You will see the Herodium, a complex of palaces with a bathhouse, a pool house, and other structures, constructed on top of a human-made hill seven and a half miles outside of Jerusalem.

I built fortresses, theaters, amphitheaters, water supply systems, and harbors. I built the entire port city of Caesarea, including markets, wide roads, baths, temples, storerooms and a palace—for me, of course—on a promontory jutting out into the sea. It even had a decorative pool. For the city's breakwaters, I imported over 24,000 cubic meters of volcanic ash from Italy—forty-four shiploads of 400 tons each. My workers quarried 12,000 cubic meters of both local stone and lime to mix with the ash to make the underwater cement for those breakwaters. I could go on and on about Caesarea alone.

Herod the Great! That's me. That *was* me . . . until it all started to unravel. You know the story. Wise men from the East came to me, the king of Judea, the king of the Jews, asking, "Where is the child who has been born king of the Jews? For we observed his star in the east and have come to pay him homage" (Matthew 2:2).

Can you imagine! Coming to me, the king of the Jews, for directions to a *new* king of the Jews so they can pay *him* homage? They should have been tripping over their robes to bow down in homage to *me!* I could've had them killed on the spot for their insolence. I should've.

Can you even comprehend how insulted I felt? This would be like going to the home of, oh I don't know, what's his name, Roger Federer, and asking him to refer you to a really great tennis player. This would be like going to that cellist, that one you all seem to like, Yo-Yo Ma, and saying, "Hey, where can I go to hear the best cello player in the world?" This would be like going to Egypt, walking up the pyramids, and asking the locals for directions to a really impressive monument. This would be like going to the sun and asking directions to the source of daylight.

That moment, that visit from those "wise men from the East" as you call them, was my undoing. I sensed the threat. I always do. When my own sons turned against me, I had them killed. When my wife turned against me, I had her and her whole family killed. I could do that. I had the power and I had no qualms about using it. Besides, I had nine other wives. It didn't matter to me.

I plotted against that "newborn king of the Jews." I feigned interest and enthusiasm for the child. "When you have found him," I told the men, "bring me word so that I may also go and pay him homage" (Matthew 2:8). What I meant was, bring me word so that I can have him killed. Of course, I didn't say that out loud.

I thought those wise men were fools, but they made a fool of me. After they found the child, they went home another way. They went home without telling me. From that day forward, I couldn't shake the feeling that this child would be my undoing.

Christmas—I did everything I could to ruin it. I did everything I could to eradicate it from the collective memory before it could take root. I ordered all the baby boys under the age of two to be slaughtered. Even that wasn't enough to silence that persistent inner voice telling me that no matter how many palaces I built, no matter how many structures I put my name on, I was nothing and I was nobody in relation to this newborn peasant baby.

My grandeur unraveled before my eyes. Or was it I that unraveled? I looked around at everything I'd built and somehow I knew that, if this child should live, my accomplishments would turn to rubble. They'd become the relics of history books, of interest only to archaeologists and gawking tourists. If this child were to live, his legacy—I sensed—would be a living, breathing thing, a worldwide movement, a force for good that would henceforth cast my greatness as folly.

What Christmas means to me is that while I may have monuments, he will have communities. I may be remembered, but he will be worshiped. I may have had power over peoples' lives, but he will have their hearts. And he won't use any of my tactics. No threats, no bribes, no intrigue, no show of force. He'll win them some other way that I don't even understand. He won't overpower them. They will freely give themselves over to him and call him Lord, Savior, Master, Teacher, and they will serve him by their own choice more willingly and more joyfully than any slave or favored servant of mine has ever served me.

What Christmas means to me is the beginning of the end of tyranny as a legitimate form of earthly rule. The child born in Bethlehem will be powerful in his weakness, and that is something that simply shakes me to my core. He will lead by serving. He will kneel before his own subjects. He will do their dirty work, and he will triumph.

They will love him. His kingdom will grow. Mine will implode.

They will create music and art to show their devotion. At Christmastime, they will sing songs, one after another after another, all about him. *Him!* I'll only appear in one verse of one carol. It's like I'm a raging mass murderer or something.

What Christmas means to me is my demise. It is the black mark on my magnificent career. It is the thing that ruined my reputation, that cast me as history's bad guy. I'm known for being duped by the wise men. I'm called paranoid, raging, merciless.

Christmas showed me the limits of my influence. It put me in my place—which hitherto nobody else had ever managed to do. I couldn't get my way with that Jesus, and I always get my way. I always leverage people and situations for my own benefit. I secure my control over others. That didn't work with him. He lived.

I have a certain disdainful respect for this child that was my undoing. Nobody else ever managed to penetrate the shell of my ego the way he did. I held Judea in my hand with an iron grip. He danced all over that. He turned my name from famous to infamous. Only one person in the Bible grew to be more loathed than I am by followers of this man; only Judas is hated more than I.

But Judas never had the glory, honor, power, dominion, and authority that I held—I was the king of the Jews, remember? Christmas took that and so much more away from me and from all tyrants everywhere, forever.

They call him Emmanuel which, if you don't know, means "God-with-us." How do you compete with God? You don't. Even Herod the Great is a nobody next to the Christ child in the manger. That is why I will always hate Christmas. It gave people a choice: him or me. They chose him.

Let me tell you a secret. It is my deepest, darkest secret. I don't blame them.

Truly yours,

Herod the (not so) Great

Prayer of Confession

Gracious God, I confess that I like to think of myself as an exemplary Christian. When I hear the story of Christ's birth, I identify with the shepherds in their enthusiasm or with the wise men in their devotion. I fail to recognize all the times that I am more like King Herod. I assert my need for control at the expense of others and cling to the security of privilege, rather than standing up for the oppressed. I uphold the status quo despite the harm it brings to the innocent. Lord God, in your mercy, forgive me. Change my heart, so that I might change my ways, and grant me your peace. Amen.

Questions for Reflection

Herod's acquisition of power and his colossal building projects earned him the title, Herod the Great. In the scriptures, the words, "He will be great" are used of John the Baptist and Jesus alike in their annunciation stories (see Luke 1:11-15 and Luke 1:30-32).

1. What does greatness signify in our culture today? Who are some of the people we call great and what do we mean by that?
2. Compare the greatness of Herod to the greatness of John the Baptist and the greatness of Jesus himself. What do you conclude from these comparisons?
3. What does the Christmas story have to say to us today on the subject of greatness?
4. "What Christmas means to me is the beginning of the end of tyranny as a legitimate form of earthly rule," says Herod in his letter. In what ways is this true? In what ways is this truth still a long way off?

Journaling Prompts

1. What do Herod and I have in common?
2. What ugly aspects of myself are exposed as Jesus takes the spotlight in the Christmas story?
3. What must I do to be great? Reflect on Matthew 20:26-28.

Closing Prayer

Holy and Eternal God, as I await the day when your promises are fulfilled, may my hopes for your coming kingdom echo your hopes. Challenge me to recognize the path for me to follow. Keep me faithful in preparing a world that reflects your priorities. Amen.

CHAPTER TWO

Beyond Me
A Letter from Elizabeth

Luke 1:24-25 & 39-45, 57-58
and Proverbs 31:10-31

DEAR CURIOUS READER:

I wasn't there for the birth of Jesus, but I didn't need to be. I guess you could say I celebrated Christmas early. If you think I'm referring to the miraculous birth of my own son, John, I'm not. While that was the happiest day of my life, I'm talking about something else. I'm thinking about a private conversation that took place months earlier, while I was still pregnant, when my kinswoman, Mary, came for a visit.

You probably haven't heard my part of the story as often as you've heard hers, so I'll fill you in. First, I'm as Jewish as they get. Both my father and my husband come from a long line of priests descended from Aaron himself, brother of Moses. For as long as anyone can remember, only the descendants of Aaron have been allowed into the

holiest places in the Temple. They alone preside over the religious ceremonies that purify the nation in God's sight. The responsibility of
teaching God's statues to each new generation rests squarely on their
shoulders.

As a woman raised by a priest, who then married a priest, I have
adhered to the ritual and moral laws of Judaism publicly and privately
throughout my entire life. I was the epitome of a godly woman—the
"woman of strength" from Proverbs 31—with one exception. My children did not "rise up and call [me] happy" (v. 28). That's because I had
no children, not even a daughter.

Even though it takes two to tango, as they say, I'm the one that
people called "barren" (Luke 1:7). My husband, Zechariah, suffered
alongside me, but he also blamed me as men of our culture were
wont to do. The truth is, I blamed myself. I didn't know any better.
The sorrow of infertility weighed on each of us, but the stigma was
mine alone.

I wept with each month's bleeding, a Passover in reverse, as if God
had marked my doorframe with something darker than blood then
ordered the angel of life to visit every bed but ours, to open every
womb but mine. With each month's disappointment, our lovemak-
ing lost more of its youthful passion. Our efforts grew desperate, then
perfunctory. They ended altogether when my bleeding stopped.

Friends and neighbors kept their distance at the market or while
drawing water from the well. They grew quiet when I approached,
then resumed their gossip when they thought I was out of earshot.
"Poor Zechariah," they would say, shaking their heads and speculating
on what secret sins of mine had brought God's disfavor.

Those who didn't shun me said unhelpful things like, "I just know
you'll get pregnant," or "You deserve it," or "Just have faith." The pious
were quick to remind me how Sarah gave birth to Isaac, and Hannah to Samuel. Oh, *please*! I came to hate those two stories. Hearing

them made me feel worse, not better. Their happy endings rubbed my own failure in my face. Besides, what happened to those women was exceptional. The sons they bore went on to make history. I was just an ordinary wife of an ordinary priest, and all I wanted was an ordinary baby. To compare my situation with theirs was silly, grandiose, and just plain maddening.

Then one day, Zechariah arrived home from the Temple acting strange. For one thing, he wasn't speaking. Stranger still, he stroked my cheek, took my hand, brought me to our bed.

Each day after that was a miracle of its own. In the mornings, I threw up. I slept through the afternoons like a bear in winter. My sagging breasts swelled. My neighbors couldn't stop themselves from touching my belly. When they plied me for details, I just said, "This is what the Lord has done for me when he looked favorably on me and took away the disgrace I have endured among my people" (Luke 1:25). They switched from gossiping about me to gossiping about Zechariah. Why had God opened *my* womb but closed *his* mouth? That was their new question.

My new question—well, more of a prayer than a question—was, "Now what?" The God I loved so dearly had surprised me month after month of my married life with bitter disappointment. Then, when all hope was gone and I prayed only for the grace to accept my lot in life, that same God had surprised me by reversing course. Would there be more surprises? "Please, God, no," I begged. I'd had enough surprises for a lifetime. All I wanted was to lie low and stay pregnant.

Then, without warning, my kinswoman Mary burst through the door having traveled eight days from Nazareth. At the sound of her greeting, the child in my belly kicked up a dance like you wouldn't believe! The earth moved. Lightning struck. My body trembled, a sounding bell. My past sorrow and present joy shrank to the size of a beetle. Something lifted me—a bird? God's spirit?—out of my small life up into the highest heavens and showed me, for a moment, the grand sweep of human existence. Then, I hurtled back down, back into my own skin again but with new eyes—eyes to see God growing in the womb of the world. Mary's greeting and the moments that followed were my Christmas.

God, who had opened my womb, now opened my mouth. I heard the sound of my own voice pronouncing God's blessing on Mary. "Blessed are you among women, and blessed is the fruit of your womb!" (Luke 1:42). Blessing is what prophets do, but there I was, doing it, not even bothering to lower my voice. I spoke with an authority I'd only ever heard from a man. "Blessed is she who believed that there would be a fulfillment of what was spoken to her by the Lord," (Luke 1:45).

I spoke as if I understood the meaning of events unfolding in real time. I gave Mary her proper title, "the mother of my Lord" (Luke 1:43). I spoke the truth: I was carrying my *baby*, but she was carrying my *Lord*. Mary and I were the first to grasp the sacred enormity of her circumstances, and I was the first to put it into words.

For someone who did not want any more surprises, I astonished myself. For someone who wanted to escape all further attention from God and melt into the invisible ordinariness afforded to a woman in my station, here I was blowing my cover, making a racket, using my outside voice, and startling myself with words that poured from me as if of their own accord.

Was I, Elizabeth, speaking for God? Or was this crazy talk? Was I old, pregnant, and confused? Or was I old, pregnant, and filled with the Holy Spirit? Did Christmas make me a prophet or a madwoman?

My exemplary Jewish upbringing taught me that, if God was anything, God was pure holiness. If God lived anywhere in the world, God lived in the Temple where priests like my husband, Zechariah, protected the purity of God from the impurity of humans and vice versa. Nothing could be more preposterous or more of an insult to God's holiness than to imagine God small, wet, soaked in bodily fluids, practically smothered in female flesh. Yet, here stood my inexplicably pregnant kinswoman, "the mother of my Lord." From my lips to God's ears.

If God wanted someone to bless Mary, God had plenty of eligible men to tap for the job: rabbis, priests, scribes, and pharisees. If God was really going through with this strange business of incarnation, shouldn't there be a priest involved? Or was that the whole point? Did God silence Zechariah to sideline him, to show that priests wouldn't be needed in quite the same way from now on? Maybe God doesn't want to be protected from our impurities. Maybe God delights to inhabit our world unmediated—up close and personal, embodied.

If God has ever planted a wild notion in your head that you simply can't let go of, then you know what Christmas means to me. It means disbelief and belief mingled together. When I say "disbelief," I don't mean doubt. I mean that exploding feeling that is more than amazement. I mean the terror you feel when everything you think you know dissolves and reconstitutes itself into its truest form, showing its true colors, none of which you've ever seen before. It's as if a rainbow faded to gray, then streaked back out across the sky in an explosion of new colors that no eye has seen nor mind conceived—more colors than violet, indigo, blue, green, yellow, orange, and red in all their permutations and combinations. It's as if there are colors you can't even imagine, but all of a sudden, you see them—disbelief and belief, commingled.

Six months into my pregnancy, all seemed to be going well. Take the ordinary joy of any woman expecting a child and multiply it by the number of years Zechariah and I silently suffered and you will sense how I was feeling that morning when Mary crossed my threshold. In a word—wonderful. And *then* Christmas happened. Mary opened my door. God opened my mouth. The simple joy I'd been feeling drained away. In its place, I felt something beyond joy, if there is such a thing. A greater miracle by far than the one being wrought in my belly was underway. The mother of my Lord stood before me. Here, in real time, was a mighty act of God. It's as if God had wrenched the Temple off its foundations, lifted it, tilted it, and poured out holiness on all flesh. It's as if God so loved the world that the two were expecting a child—a child who would be our undoing and our salvation.

What Christmas means to me is beyond me. It includes me but is not about me. It is a story to which I belong, but it is not my story. It's God's story. I didn't witness the actual birth of Christ. I didn't need to. God had already taken up residence in fetal form in the belly of a woman—a distant cousin of mine barely beyond puberty—when the fetus in my womb kicked up a dance like he'd never danced before. At that moment, the holy and the human were already mingling, enfleshed, like nothing our scriptures had attested to in times past, like nothing the world would ever see or know again.

"Why has this happened to me?" I asked, not for an explanation but in wonder (Luke 1:43). I can't begin to know. But it happened, all of it, to me, a woman. And it happened to Mary, also a woman. God entrusted us with a great deal of responsibility at Christmastime. God relied on women's wombs, women's mouths, women's voices, women's courage, women's bodies, women's ways of knowing, women's relationships, and women's faith to get a mission critical job done right.

Christian artists like to paint me kneeling humbly before Mary and always with my mouth closed. Why don't they stand me up in their portraits and place my hands on Mary's head for a blessing? Why don't they paint my open mouth? My loud voice?

When I said to Mary, "Blessed is she who believed there would be a fulfillment of what was spoken to her by the Lord," (Luke 1:45), I wonder if I was also talking to myself, trying to convince myself that God could speak through me. I wonder if I was also speaking to women of faith more generally. Perhaps I was speaking to you. I'd like to believe God loosened my tongue in order for you to loosen yours.

Yours Faithfully,

Elizabeth

Prayer of Confession

God of surprise and abundance, I confess that I do not live with the spiritual openness of Elizabeth. Forgive me for all the times I have missed opportunities to feel joy, bless others, and speak your truth. Change my mindset so that I may change my ways. I pray in Christ's name. Amen.

Questions for Reflection

1. Read Luke 1:24-25, 39-45, and 57-58. Which do you perceive to be the greater miracle: God opening Elizabeth's womb or God opening Elizabeth's mouth?

2. One Hebrew translation of the name Elizabeth is "God's promise." Another is, "My God is generous." Re-read the scripture selections from Luke 1, substituting each of these translations for the name Elizabeth and for the pronouns that refer to her. What do you notice?

3. Dr. Pascale Allotey, a researcher for a 2023 report from the World Health Organization on assisted reproductive technology, says that infertility is "a major and a widespread health

issue affecting a staggering 1 in 6 people globally over the duration of their reproductive lives." For infertile couples, Bible stories where God shows favor by granting miracle babies often don't land well. Not having children, for whatever reason, can be especially painful at Christmas, given the child-centered, home-and-family vibe of the holiday season in our culture. How might we talk about the incarnation and celebrate Christmas in ways that don't heap more pain on those who are quietly suffering?

4. This letter portrays Elizabeth as being alert to God's surprises, wary of them, and ultimately overjoyed by the sacred enormity of her Christmas moment with Mary. What, if anything, is surprising about Christmas as we celebrate it today? Where, if anywhere, do we experience the sacred enormity of the Incarnation?

5. A devout Jewish person steeped in the religious and cultural norms of her day, Elizabeth experiences divine inspiration and holy happenings in her own home. Name some of the reasons she could have discounted her experience as something unremarkable. How do you listen for God? How do you recognize a holy moment when it is happening?

Journaling Prompts

1. "What Christmas means to me is beyond me," Elizabeth writes. What do you think is meant by this statement? In what ways does the Incarnation touch you personally? In what ways does it take you out of yourself into something larger?

2. Have you ever had a spiritual experience that you struggled to explain rationally? In which "belief and disbelief mingled

together"? Or has God "ever planted a wild notion in your head that you simply can't let go of"? Describe your experience and include as many details as possible. Where do you see parallels between your story and Elizabeth's early Christmas with Mary?

3. The biblical portrait of Elizabeth shows us a woman who experiences several kinds of flourishing in her later years. Is there an Elizabeth in your own life? Someone who is spiritually alert, who is open to new discoveries, who embodies a generative spirit at an age when others are content to slow down? Are you an Elizabeth? What relationships in your life contribute to your flourishing? What is one thing you will do this week or this month to nurture one of these relationships?

4. In this story, the elder Elizabeth blesses the younger Mary (1:42, 45). If you are in your later years, write a blessing for your younger self. If you are in your younger years, write a blessing for your older self.

Closing Prayer

God, who opened the womb and the mouth of Elizabeth, open my heart to your heart. Open my spirit to your Spirit. Open my eyes to your presence. Open my hands to receive what you give. Break the hard shell of my world weariness that I may flourish here, now, and to the end of my days. Let Christmas happen for me here and now, come what may. Amen.

CHAPTER THREE

Standing and Pointing
A Letter from John the Baptist

Luke 1:5-25, 3:1-22

HELLO OUT THERE! HELLO TO ANYONE WHO HAS EARS TO HEAR!

What does Christmas mean to me? Are you talking about *your* Christmas? Christmas the way you do it, in the twenty-first century, American style? If you are, then, I'll be blunt. Ninety-nine percent of what you do for Christmas just mystifies me. I don't get it. That really shouldn't be a surprise coming from the guy who ate locusts and wild honey in the desert while wearing a camel-hair shirt. Possessions, money, fine clothes, I didn't want any of that in my own day, so why would I be impressed with those things today?

To be honest, I'm disturbed by what you call Christmas. Shopping, shopping, and more shopping. Overspending. Overeating. Overscheduling. Call me the Grinch if you must, but my heart's not too small. That's not my problem. Maybe that's your problem.

Why do you even care what Christmas means to me? I don't. My personal feelings about Christmas are irrelevant. I'd rather you ask what Christmas means for our life together as God's people. My answer to that question: everything! Christmas radically realigns every detail of every motivation behind every action in every relationship in every area of our common life, from the mundane to the sublime. And if it doesn't, it should.

To be clear, when I say Christmas, I mean *Jesus*. In my mind, the words are interchangeable. For you, Christmas is a day on the calendar. For me, Christmas is the arrival of my cousin, Jesus, and it is the entirety of his essence. Christmas is Jesus, and Jesus is Christmas, so don't get me started on your reindeer games, elves on shelves, or that "Santa Baby" song. Don't talk to me about sugar plum fairies, the North Pole, chestnuts roasting on open fires, sleigh rides, or the whole lot of it. Honestly. Have any of you ever opened a Bible?

You think I'm harsh. Perhaps that's true. I prefer the term "blunt." I know how I sound when I get wound up about something I care about. I can't help it. It's who I am. People either love me for it or they run the other way. God gave me many gifts and holding my tongue wasn't one of them. That said, I mean no harm. If I could be more like Jesus, that would be great. But I can't, because I'm me, not him. He irritated me to no end when we were kids. Too much time around that younger cousin of mine and I would start wanting to kick things. Jealousy, I guess. I was immature, a hothead. But as we grew, something shifted. I'm not sure if I changed, or if he changed me, but I came to love him—fiercely.

Here's the thing about Jesus: If you spend five minutes with the guy, if you give him five minutes of your undivided attention, you'll start wanting to get your s#!t together in the worst way. You'll be on your knees in prayer for the rest of the week and glad of it.

That's the kind of Christmas I'd like to see! If Christmas means Jesus, and Jesus means Christmas, then the right way to celebrate is for everybody to change or be changed. The right way to get ready for Christmas is to slow way down, take a pause, reflect, look inward, and reassess business as usual. Ask hard questions like, "Why do we do what we do?" Answer those hard questions honestly. Then, regroup and change whatever is messed up, make amends. And for the love of God, stop accumulating twice as much as you need, or in your case—twenty-first century Americans—twenty times as much as you need.

There is one word for all of the above: *repent*. Want to do something you'll never forget? Do that. Want to have a merry Christmas and a happy New Year? Do that.

Merry? Happy? Can those words possibly describe me, or this message from me to you? Yes, they can! Contrary to popular belief, I love what I do. I love the choices I've made. I love connecting with people at the deepest level. I love every single time that God uses my words to change someone's life. I love standing waist-deep in the river with grown men, teenagers, and grandmothers. I love pouring the water. I love that moment of recognition in their eyes, when the forgiveness grabs hold of them. They gulp for air. Anguish drains from their faces. Taking its place is something like radiance. When they cry, I cry too.

Call me crazy. Lots of people did, especially when they learned I'd walked away from the priesthood—the family business and my father's dream. That choice of mine nearly broke my dear sweet father's heart. But he and I both knew it would have been crazier for me not to leave. To me, the definition of insanity is ignoring God over and over again and expecting God to finally drop the subject. God put a fire in my belly for this weird, wonderful life of mine. I can honestly say I was born for this wilderness, for this strangeness. That's not crazy talk. That's a miracle.

Who I am is a miracle. I've known this from the beginning. There was no possible way my mother Elizabeth could have given birth at her age, but God made a joyful choice. I am that joyful choice. "You will have joy and gladness, and many will rejoice at his birth," an angel promised my father (Luke 1:14). And lo, in the manner of God doing what God promises, it came to pass. At the news of my safe and healthy delivery, neighbors and relatives flocked to my mother with warm bread, soup, bundles of herbs, and other small necessities. The women sang, fussed, and *"rejoiced with her"* (Luke 1:58). The men hung back at a respectful distance, congratulated my quiet father and offered unsolicited advice, as men do.

My parents didn't spoil me as a child, but they made sure I knew all of this. The way they studied my countenance, stroked my cheek, drank in a long last look at me before stepping out of the house for an errand, brings tears to my eyes when I think back. I was their joy and gladness. Everybody knew it, especially me. Their delight in me is *in me,* to this day. I had no children of my own, but God anointed me from birth with the oil of gladness. I was as proud of my camel hair shirt as my father had been of his priestly vestments. I wore it with joy, as "a mantle of praise" (Isaiah 61:3).

Strange as it may sound, I enjoyed raging against injustice and calling for repentance under the hot desert sun. "The voice of one crying in the wilderness" was the voice of a miracle, the voice of one born in joy solely for the joy of the Lord, the voice of a promise fulfilled and being fulfilled (Luke 3:4). I spoke from the heart. In my preaching, I honored all that I had ever known. The outpouring of God's grace was all I had ever known, and I was convinced that was what God wanted everyone to know, too. For that to be the case, everybody had to want that, too. They had to want it for themselves and for one another. And in order to want it, they'd have to wake up from whatever daze they were in and get with the program, God's program. Somebody needed to wake them up. Somebody with a big mouth and an even bigger heart. Somebody like me.

I offered "a baptism of repentance for the forgiveness of sins" (Luke 3:3), and—surprisingly—the crowds responded. I called a sin a sin and exposed the elephant in the room. I cut through the collective denial and demanded people take a fierce inventory of their actions. "What, then, should we do?" they asked, quivering with remorse. "Whoever has two coats must share with anyone who has none," I answered, "and whoever has food must do likewise." To the tax collectors, I said, "Collect no more than the amount prescribed for you." To the soldiers, I said, "Do not extort money from anyone by threats or false accusation, and be satisfied with your wages" (Luke 3:10-14).

"Prepare the way of the Lord!" was my refrain (Luke 3:4). The Lord was on the move! I can't say I had the whole picture straight in my mind, but something big was going on. I was sure of it. I had a sense of the enormity—but not the entirety—of what God was doing. The situation was urgent, and all the arrows pointed straight to my cousin, Jesus.

We were both miracle babies, both biological impossibilities. God had a claim on both of us from day one. Growing up, we'd had each other to manage the strangeness. If we heard it once, we heard it a thousand times—how the Holy Spirit whizzed around from one parent to the next to get us properly announced and properly born. We shared the burden of specialness and the curiosity it aroused. We could talk Torah together, Jesus and I, endlessly and in as much excruciating detail as our friends talked about fishing or hunting or girls.

We both became itinerant preachers as adults, and we both modeled our preaching after the same ancient prophets who called for justice to roll down like waters and for righteousness to be like an ever-flowing stream. Isaiah intrigued us to no end. Elijah was our hero. We were a bit like twins in the sense that you couldn't really know one of us unless you knew both of us. But we were not at all like twins in another sense.

If that wasn't crystal clear to me growing up, it became clear the day I looked up from my preaching on the riverbank and saw him walking toward me. I watched him wait his turn in a long line. My heart pounded in my chest. Surely, he hadn't come seeking baptism. Surely, he wasn't looking for repentance and forgiveness of sins! I'd never once caught Jesus doing something wrong as a child, not once. Had he snapped, I wondered. Had he gone and done something egregious without me noticing? No, that was impossible. But there he was, kneeling at my feet, asking to be baptized. Asking me to baptize him.

I have never felt angrier, not before or since. "No!" I cried. "I can't. I won't. Of the two of us, you are the greater by far!" I told him, "I need to be baptized by you, and do you come to me?" (Matthew 3:14). I heard myself shouting for him to get up, go away, leave now. But Jesus wouldn't take no for an answer. The look in his eyes settled the matter. He would simply have to be baptized. That's what made him great—his insistence on being less. You might say that was my Christmas moment, Jesus kneeling at water's edge, eyes trained on me, asking, insisting, waiting for my consent.

In our day, people compared us with each other. They confused us with each other. Some thought he was the prophet Elijah returned, and others thought I was. Some called us competitors, and others said we were as alike as alike can be. They were wrong, all of them. I spoke powerfully and persuasively, but his preaching changed the world. I spoke for God with wisdom and insight, but he spoke *as* God. I told the truth. He was the truth. We both took risks, made enemies, and got ourselves killed as a result. But only one of us rose from the grave to finish what he started, to trample down death, and overcome evil with good once and for all.

That one isn't me. Compared with him, I'm . . . I'm not . . . worthy, not even to untie the sandals on his feet. He is all good all the time. I hated him for that as a kid, but I don't now. Nor do I feel an ounce of shame. What I do feel is what I've always felt from my parents, from God, joy and gladness.

Think of me the way you might think of one of those wacky inflatable air dancers outside a car dealership. They may be annoying, but they get people to stop and take notice. I'm here to do that. To get you and everyone else to stop racing around on your Christmas hamster wheels, to get you to take notice and study what I—wacky inflatable air dancer—am pointing toward. Here, people of God, is the one you want to be chasing. The one who doesn't need any chasing. Don't be a hamster, or a lemming, or an idiot. See, here is the one who came to redeem and restore.

And I will stand here, as I am doing now, and I will point to Jesus, for as long as it takes the world to notice. If I have to keep standing and pointing until the end of time, then that's what I'll do, with joy and gladness.

Sincerely,

John the Baptist

Prayer of Confession

Big-hearted God, who calls men and women to live out the courage of their convictions with abandon, I confess my hardheartedness. I am not brave like John, nor do I want to be. I am sullen when I could be joyful. I give in to social pressures instead of speaking the truth with love. You lead me in paths of righteousness, but I choose the hamster wheel instead. This Christmas, create in me a clean heart and renew a right spirit in me. I pray in Christ's name. Amen.

Questions for Reflection

1. Both Jesus and John the Baptist were influenced by the ancient prophets who called for justice and repentance. Compare the preaching of John the Baptist to the preaching of Jesus in the following passages. What do you notice?

John the Baptist	Jesus
Luke 3:1-6	Matthew 5:1-12, Matthew 20:16
Luke 3:7-9	Matthew 5:38-48
Luke 3:10-14	Luke 6:27-36

2. This letter portrays John the Baptist as big-hearted and joyful. Do you think of him this way? Why or why not?

3. Think about the ways you will be preparing for Christmas and note the holiday events on your calendar. Imagine John the Baptist tagging along with you for all of them. How would he feel? How would you feel with him there?

Journaling Prompts

1. What decisions are you facing as the holiday season gets into full swing? What decisions are you facing in your personal life? Write about one of these decisions and imagine yourself making a joyful choice, in the spirit of this letter.

2. Choose a secular Christmas character—the Grinch, Santa Claus, Clara from the Nutcracker ballet, Frosty the Snowman, Virginia, anybody—and write an imagined dialogue

between that character and John the Baptist as he is portrayed
in this letter.

3. Keep John the Baptist in mind as you go about decorating
your home and your Christmas tree for the season. Select or
create a decoration to represent John the Baptist. Write a letter to John the Baptist, telling him what you've selected, why,
and what meaning it holds for you.

Closing Prayer

Holy God, make me bold like John the Baptist and a little bit weird.
Holy Jesus, help me be that person who helps every other person
stop, notice, and be astonished. Holy Spirit, sweep me along in the
blessed rush toward that day when all flesh shall see the salvation of
God. Amen.

CHAPTER FOUR

Being Quiet for a Change
A Letter from Zechariah

Luke 1:5-24, 39-80 and Numbers 18:1-7

DEAR PILLARS OF THE CHURCH AND DEAR REBELS:

A child, at last! John was God's Christmas gift to me, and with the birth of John came the rebirth of a dream. It was a dream I'd coiled up and tucked away years earlier, a dream of incense and offerings, of tunics, robes, and ephod, a dream of anointing oil, gold lamps, sacred fire, blood, and prayers, a dream of a child come of age—flesh of my flesh—clothed in sacred garb, kneeling before the elders for the laying on of hands.

Child and dream came swaddled together in a bundle the midwife placed in my arms after Elizabeth's arduous labor. I cradled him with the practiced care of one accustomed to handling holy objects of great worth. One day this son of mine would be a priest like me, like my father before me, and his father before him. Soon enough, when the child was weaned, I would bring him with me to the Temple, kindle his sacred wonder by my example, and bask in the pride in his eyes at the prospect of following in my footsteps.

"He will be great in the sight of the Lord," an angel had promised me in a private, holy moment even before Elizabeth conceived (Luke 1:15). I spent many a private moment after that wondering what those words meant. Would John, "with the spirit and power of Elijah" (Luke 1:17), surpass my rank in service to God? Would he impress and earn the respect of the Jerusalem elite? Would they elevate a poor priest from the hill country of Judea above their own brothers and cousins to serve as high priest?

I will admit that I compared myself to our first ancestor Abraham. John was my Isaac, my "joy and gladness" (Luke 1:14), a divine promise fulfilled. I compared Elizabeth to Hannah, whom the Lord remembered in a similar fashion with the birth of Samuel. John was our Samuel, designated for an exceptionally rigorous holy life imbued with God's Spirit.

Even our names suggested as much. Zechariah means "God remembers." Elizabeth means "God's promise." John means "God is gracious." String the three of us together, and we form a sentence, a declaration: God remembers God's promises and God is gracious. What gracious acts might God accomplish through my son, the priest, for the welfare of our people? Would all our work to rebuild God's trust in our nation finally restore us to our former glory as an independent nation ruled by a descendent of David? This was every priest's dream, and with wondrous events unfolding around me, it began to seem entirely possible.

I had plenty of time to think about such things, because Christmas—or at least my part in the Christmas story—left me no choice. I lost my voice. I was the first person on the scene in the Gospel of Luke, but what did I add to the action? Nothing at all, until the very end. I asked one question, *one*, and for that, God's angel shut my mouth and handed the speaking parts over to Elizabeth until the kid was born and circumcised.

It was just one question. I've replayed that memory in my head a million times while searching the scriptures. The Torah is filled with people questioning God and God's messengers. Why couldn't I? Sarah laughed outright when an angel said she would have a son. Moses objected not once, not twice, but three times when God sent him to Pharaoh. Jeremiah protested, "Ah, Lord God! Truly I do not know how to speak, for I am only a boy" (Jeremiah 1:6).

Then there are the Psalms. People hurl questions at God left and right, accusing, cajoling, and demanding answers. We sang these psalms at the Temple, and I know what they say. How long, Lord? Why, Lord? How could you, Lord? All I asked was one simple question, just "How will I know that this is so? For I am an old man, and my wife is getting on in years" (Luke 1:18). I'd brought so many questions to God before in prayer, and God never seemed to mind. Why now? Was my question an honest one, or was it disbelief in disguise? Maybe it was both.

In any case, Christmas made me quiet for a change. I'd never been at a loss for words before, but now I could offer none, no suggestions, no learned commentary, no quotations from the Torah. A funny thing happens when all you can do is observe and listen. What happens is—you *do* observe and you *do* listen. I want to describe it all for you exactly as I remember it . . .

The moment Mary arrives at our door, singing out her greeting. The wordless, knowing look that passes from one woman to the other. The way my dear Elizabeth's hand darts to her belly and rests there. The eloquence with which she then speaks: "Blessed is she who believed there would be a fulfillment of what was spoken to her by the Lord" (Luke 1:45). Each word uttered as if she, not I, were the priest in the family, as if the authority to speak on God's behalf resided in her!

Then the younger's reply as she shared an even greater prophecy, "My soul magnifies the Lord and my spirit rejoices in God my Savior, for he has looked with favor on the lowly state of his servant . . . He has come to the aid of his child Israel, in remembrance of his mercy, according to the promise he made to our ancestors" (Luke 1:46-48, 54-55).

Mute though I was, my jaw dropped. Part of me wanted to snap at them both, wanted to instruct them not to say another word and scold them both for presuming to speak as only men were permitted. Another part of me wanted to drop to my knees, ask for a blessing, and ordain them both to the priesthood then and there!

I could do neither, and so God kept the spotlight where it belonged, on them. My original question to the angel, "How will I know?" answered itself. In the strangest of role reversals, my wife and her young kinswoman became my teachers. When, at last, my voice was restored, all I could do was confirm and amplify everything they had already said to connect their pregnancies with God's enduring grace.

When I could finally talk again, I spoke more than I knew, and for a know-it-all like me, that is saying a lot.

> Thus [the Lord] has shown the mercy promised to our
>   ancestors,
>   and has remembered his holy covenant,
> the oath that he swore to our ancestor Abraham,
> to grant us that we, being rescued from the hands of our
>   enemies,
> might serve him without fear, in holiness and righteousness
>   in his presence all our days. (Luke 1:72-75)

When Jesus was born just a few months after John, I suppose we thought things would settle down, but Christmas didn't end there.

This was only the first chapter in a long story filled with more ups, downs, and rocky patches than the hill country of Judea.

Hidden in the bottom corner of the intricately carved chest that held the silks and jewelry of Elizabeth's dowry, I kept my most cherished possession—a faded and frayed sash worn by the men in our family on the day of their consecration as priests. Some nights, after a good day of teaching, when John had shown particular zeal and aptitude for God's law, I would reach into the chest, uncoil the sash, run it through my fingers and tremble with excitement at the thought of tying it around his waist on the day of his anointing.

But this future was not to be. My big-hearted son grew up to be stubborn and unyielding. He called himself principled, but I thought him naive. He loved what I loved about the Temple but could not turn a blind eye to the unlovely parts. He was too intelligent to not notice how the powers that be steered the Temple's wealth toward the Jerusalem priests and left the priests in the hill country, priests like me, with barely enough to put food on our tables.

It was an open secret that our religious leaders traded favors with the Roman authorities. In vain, I tried to explain to John that kowtowing to Rome was our only choice. "Herod the Great wasn't all bad," I argued. "Look what he did to expand and beautify the Temple!" The Temple complex was now twice its original size, and the Temple itself had been elevated, enlarged, and faced with white stone that glimmered in the Judean sun. Beneath its porticoes, pilgrims from far and wide could purchase the animals they needed for their required offerings. After five hundred years, our people finally had a suitably grand dwelling for God that could accommodate large numbers of worshipers from all around. "Shouldn't that count for something?" I asked John.

"Yeah, it counts for a lot," retorted John. "It keeps people like you from complaining while we pay our Temple taxes plus whatever the Roman governor extorts from us." I could only shake my head.

There would be no priestly regalia for John. He dressed in a rough garment made of camel's hair with a leather belt for a sash. The prestige of Jerusalem, with its hallowed halls and storied past, were not for him. He chose the wilderness for his ministry. He went rogue.

There would be no presiding over liturgies for John, no consecrating sacred vessels. It wouldn't be my John up front at the altar handling the burnt offerings, grain offerings, or sin offerings on behalf of the faithful multitudes. My son would not lead in any of the ways I'd taken such care to teach him. After all my Torah training, he became famous for something the Torah never even mentions. Baptism, he called it.

In today's world, you might say John was spiritual but not religious, although that's a distinction he himself would not have made. John fashioned his preaching after the prophets we'd studied together so thoroughly in his younger years—Amos, Isaiah, Jeremiah. Taking a page straight out of their playbooks, he told people to repent, change their ways, clean up their act, and do it now! But then, as if to seal the deal, he'd walk with them into the river, up to his waist, for that newfangled baptism business of his.

My son drew crowds. It seemed everybody wanted "repentance for the forgiveness of sins" (Luke 3:3b). I'm told he was quite the rock star out there by the Jordan River, bringing grown men to their knees, reducing the arrogant to fear and trembling at the reckoning to come. But for every convert, I suppose he also made an enemy. My John didn't mince words. He insulted people to their face. He called them snakes and insisted that their religious rituals and Jewish heritage meant less than nothing if they persisted in any kind of evil or injustice. He endorsed Jesus, baptizing him as the greater of the two. Then, the two egged each other on with their talk about religious hypocrisy and corruption.

The path John chose broke my heart, not once but twice. The first was when he said a firm "no" to the vocation of the priesthood. The second—the infinitely more painful—was when his fiery preaching got him killed. I've second-guessed myself long enough to know I couldn't have stopped him. Stopping him would have been wrong. But I can't help rehashing what I said and how I said it. I hope he's forgiven me.

I didn't flat out call that baptism business of his a bunch of hooey. I just laid out what I considered the facts and asked probing questions. I gently pushed, saying, "My son," I said, "you know repentance and conversion have been cardinal themes in Israel's faith since time immemorial. Surely, we agree on this central point. But there's a right way to do these things, in the Temple, with burnt offerings and grain offerings, as the Torah prescribes, with a priest, John, a duly designated priest who loves the people just as much as he loves God, presiding as a sacred intermediary between the two." I reminded him how the sins of our people once led to captivity in Babylon. I stressed how careful we must be not to repeat the mistakes of the past. "Because God remembered God's covenant with our people," I said, laying a gentle hand on his muscled shoulder, "we also must remember and observe all that God has commanded us."

On other days, I straight up argued with him. "Please, don't throw your life away! You're young. This is youthful passion. Locusts and wild honey won't keep you alive forever. Surely, you'll want to marry and have children. How will you feed and clothe them without a steady income? Think of your fine priestly family! Don't scorn us by turning your back on all that we hold sacred. Please tone down your rhetoric. You could get yourself killed!"

I'm not proud of it, but there were times I resorted to shame. "Stop thinking about yourself for a change," I said, wagging my finger in his face. "You know you were meant to be a priest from the moment of your conception. Think of your mother in her old age! The neighbors gossiped about her before you were born. Would you have them gossiping again? Think about me! This baptism business of yours is making me the laughingstock of the Temple. I'll be a pariah in my own tribe thanks to you."

I called him an ingrate and a reprobate. I shook him by the shoulders and shouted, "Just who do you think you are young man? A prophet?"

The consequences of his choices followed me wherever I went. I defended him publicly when the neighbors criticized. More than once, though, I joined my affronted colleagues in trash-talking him, until my conscience couldn't abide it and I blew up or walked away.

One day, I retrieved the sash I'd been saving for his consecration, walked over to him, and pressed it into his hands. I curled his fingers around it. Without a word, John uncurled his fingers, studied the sash, and handed it back to me. "Father," he said, his voice choking, "I love the Torah as much as you do. Believe me, Father, when I tell you the word of God came to me in the wilderness. I can no more say 'no' to God than you could have said 'no' to the angel who announced my birth."

I ran the sash through my fingers and said nothing. I returned it to the chest and closed the lid. Time to be quiet again, I said to myself, remembering the angel who'd made me mute. Time to stop thinking about myself—or stop thinking the way that I habitually think. I told myself there was a very real possibility that John could be doing exactly what God needed him to do, and that he had, in fact, grown up to be the very person I'd raised him to be. Wasn't he everything I had hoped for in a son? I studied his countenance. Wasn't he more than I could have imagined? What was it that I'd said all those years earlier when the angel finally loosened my tongue? The words came back to me: "And you, child, will be called the prophet of the Most High" (Luke 1:76).

I prayed day and night for God to keep John safe. He worried me sick. People we knew went to the river and came back asking, "Didn't we want to go hear him for ourselves?"

"So what if John didn't follow you into the priesthood?" Elizabeth said to me one day. "I see no harm in going to hear him. Why are you holding out?"

We made our decision. She packed provisions. I loaded the donkey. We made the long trek together, leaning on our walking sticks. We stopped at the edge of the crowd, close enough to hear his voice, but not close enough for him to see us.

What will happen next? Put yourself in my shoes for a moment and consider. Will the passion of John's preaching cut you to the quick? Will you find yourself wanting to show your utter devotion to God in this strangely spare but thoroughly compelling ritual of his to which so many are drawn? Will your old, arthritic legs propel you toward him as if of their own accord? Will you fight the urge? Will you yield?

And if you yield, what of it? Will John's baptism cleanse you? Pollute you? Does it signify a new beginning for you in the frailty of old age, or does it mark you as an abomination before God, a reprobate priest, the deluded father of a narcissist? Will this be the day you turn your back on so much that you and your forebears deemed sacred? Or will this be your proudest father-and-son moment, as you and John together honor all that you have ever known to be true?

I fell quiet. I made my choice. As if in a dream come true.

Yours in wonder,

Zechariah

✳ ✳ ✳

Prayer of Confession

God of Grace, I confess that I come to Christmas as I come to all things—with my own agenda and expectations. I do not greet the Holy Spirit in those who don't conform to this agenda and these expectations. I choose not to see the lines connecting my faith and theirs, connecting my life and theirs. Too often, I listen to myself and not to you. In your mercy, forgive me. Give me ears to hear and a quiet heart. I pray in Christ's name. Amen.

Questions for Reflection

1. Both Zechariah and John are devoted to God, but their devotion takes different forms. How would you describe Zechariah's devotion to God? How would you describe John the Baptist's devotion to God? Where does their faith overlap and where does it diverge? Would you say you are more of a Zechariah or more of a John the Baptist? Why?

2. This letter posits a religious conflict that is also a generational conflict between father and son. How is your faith similar to or different from that of your parents? How is your faith similar to or different from that of either your grown children, or of younger people you have taught or mentored? Where do your choices align with theirs and where do they differ? On what basis do you decide what is essential and what is optional?

3. Reflect on the Hebrew meaning of the names Zechariah ("God remembers"), Elizabeth ("God's promise"), and John ("God is gracious"). How do these Hebrew names help us tell and interpret the Christmas story? Reread Zechariah's words

when his voice returns in Luke 1:67-79 and look for echoes of the Hebrew names in what Zechariah has to say.

4. Both John and Jesus speak out against religious hypocrisy, corruption, and the unholy alliance between religious leaders and the Roman military occupation. Where do you see the church turning a blind eye to hypocrisy? How does the church safeguard against corruption? Many have said that silence in the face of oppression amounts to siding with the oppressor. Where does your church speak and where is it silent on the social justice issues of our day? What prevents churches from taking bold stances?

Journaling Prompts

1. This letter from Zechariah is full of questions. Christmas, in its fullest sense, asks us challenging questions, ultimate questions, questions that call for a decision. Reread the letter focusing on the questions it asks. Choose one of the questions that you find compelling and respond to it in your journal. Alternatively, write and respond to a Christmas question of your own.

2. Given the Bible's many examples of people questioning God, why do you suppose Zechariah is reprimanded? Compare his question (Luke 1:18) to Mary's question (Luke 1:34) in the very next scene. What questions do you have for God? Write them out. Do you feel safe asking them? Why or why not? When is a question "disbelief in disguise" and when is it an honest question? Review your questions as you consider this and cross out or rewrite any that need it.

3. With Zechariah and John the Baptist in mind, listen to a recording of the song "Father and Son" by Cat Stevens. Think of it as a Christmas carol, a song that helps tell part of the Christmas story. Choose a family member, living or dead, and write a letter to them, seeking understanding about a choice you've made or a choice they've made in the past. Be sure to write your letter in love, not bitterness. You can either choose to mail your letter or not, but bring all of this to God in prayer once you have finished.

Closing Prayer

God who remembers, help me to remember you in all I do this Christmas season and beyond. God who keeps promises, help me to be as steadfast as Zechariah and as bold as John the Baptist. God of grace, when I fail to see you, shut my mouth. When I fail to hear you, shut my mouth. Give me quiet time this Christmas season, so that by listening, I might grow in faith and joyfully change my ways. Amen.

CHAPTER FIVE

A Summons
A Letter from Isaiah of Jerusalem

Isaiah 2:2-4, 6:1-8, 7:14,
9:2-7, and 11:1-9

DEAR PEOPLE WHO LIVE IN ANXIOUS TIMES:

I'm the guy with fire in my belly. I'm the guy who can't keep still and who won't shut up. I'm the relative at the dinner table who dominates the conversation—the dreamer, the odd duck, the curmudgeon. I'm the guy who's hard to argue with because he has a way with words and he knows his stuff. I'm the guy you want on your side but can never persuade, can never budge, not even an inch, from his principled convictions. Add religious zeal to the mix and you'll have a pretty good idea of what to expect when you ask for my opinion.

I am Isaiah of Jerusalem and I'm the outlier in this collection of letters about the whole "What Christmas means to me" question. You see, I'd been dead a good 700 years before the birth of Jesus. What you now call Christmas was the furthest thing from my mind in the eighth century BCE when I tried—and sadly failed—to get the kingdom of Judah back on track in time to avert the catastrophe of exile. Writing to you now feels like déjà vu all over again. We both know your generation faces a global crisis exponentially worse than anything we imagined in our day, and you want to talk about Christmas? Well, I don't.

Not yet anyway. I want to talk about the Tigris and Euphrates rivers. They're drying up! Farmers in the fertile crescent—the very cradle of civilization where farming and irrigation first emerged 12,000 years ago—can no longer farm. The region's storied wheat fields have turned to stubble, and its people are on the move.

It is my divine obligation as a prophet to state the obvious, and so I will: these conditions in the cradle of civilization are a sign of what's to come worldwide. Does the phrase "canary in a coal mine" mean anything to you? Catastrophic climate change threatens human and animal life with mass destruction rivaling anything ever invented for warfare. Expect famine, disease, floods, wildfires, and wave upon wave of social violence born of sheer desperation. Burning fossil fuels for generations triggered this vicious cycle, and it has to stop. Christmas won't mean much of anything in the not-too-distant future if your generation fails to act. To ignore the matter would be a grave injustice to vulnerable populations around the globe, and it is an affront to God, our Creator. You have one chance to act to forestall the worst of it and that chance is now. It will not be available much longer.

The prophetic message I delivered to my own people was not terribly different from what I'm saying to you now. We faced the very real possibility of our annihilation as a people. A messy civil war had split our kingdom in two, leaving us badly weakened and vulnerable to outside aggression, but the root of the problem was our failure to honor God and one another as people of God. We went through the motions. We brought our goats and pigeons to sacrifice in the Temple, but we neglected the weightier matters of God's law—justice, compassion, love. I told Judah that if we did not address these spiritual failures swiftly and comprehensively, we risked being abandoned by God altogether, evicted from our land, and shackled in captivity to our sworn enemies.

All the religious rituals and festivals in the world wouldn't please God one whit, I told the people of Judah, if we persisted in doing whatever the heck we felt like in our day-to-day dealings. I gave voice to God's grave displeasure, asking, "What to me is the multitude of your sacrifices?" (Isaiah 1:11) and declaring, "I cannot endure solemn assemblies with iniquity" (Isaiah 1:13). God has never taken kindly to empty religiosity, not then, not now. Nor has God ever gone soft on ethics. If anything, Jesus raised the bar, calling his followers to an even higher ethical standard than before. I asked my people, what good are Torah rituals without Torah ethics? I ask you the same. What good are the rituals of Christmas without the ethic of Christmas?

Don't get me wrong, I'm not suggesting you stop celebrating. I am not speaking out against your pageants or your Chrismon trees or your lovely tradition of singing "Silent Night" at the end of your candlelight services. The rituals are not the problem unless they become an end unto themselves. By all means, keep doing what you're doing, but do it in a way that ignites your collective passion for the work, the ethics, of Christmas. Don't take your eye off the threat barreling toward you, not even for a minute. Don't think you can brush off the peculiar burden God has placed on the shoulders of your generation. Please, learn from your sacred history. The people of Judah shrugged off my prophetic warnings. They took their eye off the Assyrian juggernaut barreling down on them, and they suffered mightily. Don't make the same mistake! And remember, this time, the consequences of inaction are global.

In the year King Uzziah died, I had an honest to goodness full-blown religious experience in the inner chamber of the Temple of Jerusalem, the Holy of Holies. I felt a call that others, both before and after me, have also felt, a summons from God. God, in all holiness, blazed before me as if enthroned. I heard what could only have been the voice of God asking, " 'Whom shall I send?' and then I heard what could only have been my own voice responding, 'Here am I; send me!'" (Isaiah 6:8). I think of that mystical moment as my Christmas, my moment with Emmanuel, which means *God with us*. In God's presence, when God was with me, I experienced God's call. God called me to address a crisis. God called me to plead with a nation to change its ways. God called me to confront kings and leaders in their complacency. God called me to speak on God's behalf, to be a surrogate for God, and to adhere to the courage of my convictions, come what may.

What I experienced in a private mystical moment is what happened in public for all the world, in flesh and blood, when Christ was born in Bethlehem. Holiness blazed among mortals not for a moment but for a lifetime, and for all time. God blazed in the countenance and the words of Jesus when he taught the multitudes. God blazed in the passion with which he spoke truth to power. God blazed in his healing touch, his jovial laugh, and the quiet dignity with which he faced condemnation, suffering, and death on a cross. God blazes on in the risen Christ, with a glory brighter than a thousand suns, and all of this—all of it taken together—is what Christmas means.

But there's more! My mystical moment in God's presence had a purpose. My visit from God—my Christmas moment, as I think of it now—came with a summons. God asked, "Whom shall I send?" I view Christmas—actual Christmas—as your summons. Think of it like this: on that first Christmas, God burst out of the Holy of Holies and has been walking the earth ever since, ready to be noticed. Those who notice find themselves drawn into a deeper reverence, a clarity of purpose that is both wonderful and terrifying. Those who notice can't help but recognize God's voice as it echoes again and again, "Whom shall I send?" Christmas summons you to be a surrogate for God. I would go so far as to say that Christmas *obliges* you to do so, to the best of your ability, come what may.

Face the truth! State the obvious! In every generation, vulnerable communities have faced threats to their very survival. Now, for the first time ever, that threat to survival extends to the whole human family. The very ecosystem that sustains all of life on God's good earth is strained to the breaking point. Say these things. Say them out loud. Say them until you are blue in the face. Do not back down.

Christmas calls for responsible action steps, so begin by admitting to one another: "This is our mess. We have no one to blame but ourselves. Let's clean things up." Take responsibility, but do not be hobbled by it. Move on quickly to determine what piece of the mess is yours to untangle, and then set about to do just that. Seek God's guidance. Rely on God's help. God won't be waving a magic wand to fix things for you, but neither does God expect you to go it alone.

In Judah, we all had a share in the sorry state of affairs that threatened our existence as a nation, but those with power bore the lion's share of responsibility. In God's name I exposed judges for taking bribes, loudly proclaiming, "They do not defend the orphan, and the widow's cause does not come before them" (Isaiah 1:23). In God's name I denounced wealthy landowners and told them to stop crushing the poor who worked in their fields (Isaiah 3:15). In God's name I entered the royal chambers and pleaded with kings to use their authority responsibly. "Zion shall be redeemed by justice, and those in her who repent, by righteousness," I declared (Isaiah 1:27). But of the four kings I served, I can claim only some small success with Hezekiah. His reforms gave us hope, but with neighboring Assyria breathing down our necks, extorting tribute, and waving their idols in our faces, Hezekiah could only do so much. Instead of beating swords into plowshares and spears into pruning hooks, Hezekiah led us into yet another costly war. My career as a prophet ended with my nation in far worse shape than before. I believed exile would be next. I'm sad to say I wasn't wrong.

Let Judah's story be a cautionary tale for you. Catastrophic climate change will hurt the poor before it hurts the wealthy. It is already doing so. As with Judah, those who contributed the least to the problem stand to suffer the most. Wealthy nations and their consumer-citizens bear the lion's share of responsibility for pumping carbon into the atmosphere. Some may look to science and technological developments for a solution, others to economics, and still others to politics, but the climate crisis is at its heart a spiritual crisis. What I'm going to say next will sound harsh, but I'm going to say it anyway. If you and your generation manage to do nothing while the world God made bakes to a crisp in an oven of our own making, you might just as well spit in God's face. If enough people do nothing, there will be no punishment from God. The consequences of inaction will suffice.

If my blunt speech does not persuade you, let Christmas do the persuading. Let Christmas summon you to hope. Hope is a much better motivator than alarm, and because of Christmas, there is hope. As I said earlier, what you now call "Christmas" was the furthest thing from my mind as I served God in the eighth century BCE. I had no insider knowledge about the who, what, where and when of the big events seven centuries away. Lurching from one crisis to the next left me precious little time to speculate about the distant future. But I'd had what I now call my Christmas moment in the divine presence of God, which meant I had hope. I had hope for an exemplary king on Judah's throne who would govern with justice. I had hope that the spirit of the Lord would be upon such a king, "the spirit of wisdom and understanding, the spirit of counsel and might, the spirit of knowledge and the fear of the Lord" (Isaiah 11:2).

You need hope in your time every bit as much as I needed hope in mine. The crisis you face is far greater in scope than the crisis we were facing, but your scientists say there is still time to prevent the worst outcomes. Even more importantly, you have an advantage in the hope department because you live on the other side of Christmas. In Jesus Christ, you now have what I could only imagine. He is the Wonderful Counselor, Mighty God, Everlasting Father, and Prince of Peace. Jesus is a dream come true. We had hope in God's promises. You have hope in their fulfillment. For you, Christmas is a done deal. It's ongoing. Christ was born. Christ lives.

It is my divine obligation as a prophet to speak the truth, to point out the obvious. That holds just as true for the good news as for the bad, so let me conclude with what is good. You live in a world where Christmas is not just a date on the calendar, but a spiritual reality. This is good! Your king reigns neither as a distant memory nor as a future possibility but is enthroned now, always, and forever as the King of kings, Emmanuel, God-with-Us. This is good! The very spirit that was in him is now loose in the world for all to claim, so shout this good news from the rooftops and let that Spirit go to work in you! Help yourselves to the hope of Christmas. Harness it to support one another to take action in this present hour. Trust that Christmas has delivered—and will continue to deliver—all the hope you will ever need.

In my day, I cared very little for religious holidays and rituals of any kind. To be honest, I feel much the same way about your Christmas traditions. I have no emotional connection to the Christmas customs you've accumulated for generations. I don't care what you fix for Christmas dinner or what sort of church service your family prefers or whether you liked you prefer a real Christmas tree or an artificial one. I'm just not concerned with how you celebrate Christmas. I am concerned with the direction Christmas points you in for the remaining 364 days of the year.

There is, however, one small detail in your holiday celebrations that touches me deeply. I simply love your custom of lighting the candles on an Advent wreath in the weeks leading up to Christmas. Often, you'll read a selection from my writings as part of this ritual.

The first candle on that wreath is usually called the candle of hope. Each year, I hold my breath for the lighting of this candle. In its steady flame, the light that I knew and the light that you know burn as one. Hope burns, it blazes; it lights the way. Hope is what Christmas means to me.

Yours humbly,

Isaiah of Jerusalem

Prayer of Confession

God of Truth, I confess my reluctance to hear the truth when it implicates me. I confess that I would rather not think about catastrophic climate change right now, with so much to do to get ready for Christmas. I confess that it is more convenient for me to be overwhelmed with a problem than for me to involve myself in solutions. In your mercy, forgive these sins and all my shortcomings. Change my heart so that I may change my ways. I pray in Christ's name. Amen.

Questions for Reflection

1. The book of Isaiah is a compilation of prophetic writings from three different prophets written over a period of several hundred years. Pieces of it were written before, during, and after the Babylonian exile. Scholars refer to these three sections as First Isaiah (chapters 1–39), Second Isaiah (chapters 40–55) and Third Isaiah (chapters 56–66). This letter in this chapter is written in the voice of First Isaiah, also known as Isaiah of Jerusalem, who did not mince words in his critique of Judah. What do you make of the comparison between the crisis facing Judah and the climate crisis today? How does this letter make you feel?

2. Consider the statement, "Zion shall be redeemed by justice" (Isaiah 1:27a). How does the burning of fossil fuels that cause climate change perpetuate injustice? Who bears the brunt of suffering as the global climate crisis unfolds? How does a biblical summons to justice from the eighth century BCE apply to our present circumstances?

3. Whom do you consider to be the Isaiahs of the earth care movement today? How are their warnings received? Who inspires you the most?

4. In what ways do you consider the climate crisis to be a spiritual crisis? What are some hopeful steps you might take in response to this letter? Choose one and ask someone you know well to hold you accountable.

5. What are the implications of Isaiah's statement that we live "on the other side of Christmas"? If you were to say the words, "Today, I live on the other side of Christmas," every morning, how might that shape your day? Try it for one week and see.

Journaling Prompts

1. In this letter, Isaiah of Jerusalem says, "I view Christmas—actual Christmas—as your summons." With this in mind, look up the poem "The Work of Christmas" by Howard Thurman and read it over a few times. What, in your mind, is the real work of Christmas? What part of the work of Christmas do you feel is yours to do? In your journal, write out a Christmas call to action from God to you.

2. Do you observe Christmas as a date on the calendar or as a spiritual reality? At the top of a blank page, either in your journal or elsewhere, write "To-Do List for Celebrating Christmas as. . . ." Beneath this heading, make two columns. Label the left-hand column, "Date on Calendar" and the right-hand column, "Spiritual Reality." List the activities you typically do during the Christmas season in the corresponding column. Then, using a different color pen, brainstorm things you might do differently. Share with God the thoughts and feelings that emerge from working through this activity.

Closing Prayer

God of Christmas, as you embodied hope in the person and work of Jesus, help me to embody hope to the best of my God-given ability. Shape the words of my mouth, direct the work of my hands, and kindle the imagination of my heart. Give me this day my daily portion of hope and let it be sufficient for the tasks that are mine to accomplish. Sustain my life of service to you as you sustained Isaiah of Jerusalem in his ministry. Let Christmas be the way, and not simply a day, for me to honor your majesty, wisdom, and justice. Amen.

CHAPTER SIX

What God Brings
A Letter from the Innkeeper

Luke 2:1-7

DEAR TWENTY-FIRST-CENTURY CHRISTIANS,

I'm getting tired of being a figment of your imagination, although I am used to it at this point. The idea of me occurs to you once a year for about three seconds when you hear the story of Christmas. At your children's pageants and your outdoor live nativities, somebody dresses up in a costume, opens the door of a pretend inn, hangs a lantern on a hook, talks briefly to Mary and Joseph, then shakes his head and points out back. Then, that somebody waves goodbye and closes the door. With that, my part in your religious imagination is done for the year.

I'm writing today because you've asked what Christmas means to me, but before I get to that, I want to clear up a few things, so I'll need more than three seconds of your time. Thank you very much.

Let's start with how you view me, because that will have a big impact on our ability to communicate. Some of you view me as mean and coldhearted. You assume I made a snap judgment about a very pregnant young woman who showed up on my doorstep. You have me speaking coarsely to the young couple before waving them out back and slamming the door behind me. Others imagine the exact opposite. You give me a twinkle in my eye and a jolly double chin. You see me rushing good-naturedly back and forth from the stable on Christmas night with linens and towels and bowls of steaming broth.

Let's take a closer look at where you get your ideas of me. My entire role in the Christmas narrative comes from ten words in the Bible. Here they are, in their entirety, and I quote: "because there was no place for them in the inn" (Luke 2:7, NKJV). As you can see, I don't even appear in the Bible. There is not one single mention of me in scripture beyond this neutral statement about my jam-packed inn. From these ten words (ten words!), you and zillions of others have conjured me entirely in your own image.

Who I am in the divine drama is an ink blot. You see in me what you want to see. If you want me to be a kindly innkeeper who takes pity on Mary in her condition and Joseph in his distress, then that is what you will make of me. If you want me to be the stereotypical heartless business owner who cares only about money, money, money, then you will turn me into that guy. Either way, I'm a caricature of your own making.

Here are the facts. When it came time for Mary to deliver her child, she gave birth and laid him in a manger, my manger. I offered something to Mary and Joseph and to Jesus as well, something essential: shelter, warmth, and a reasonably safe, private space for a pregnant woman—and total stranger—to have her baby. And, unlike the rest of the Christmas gang in your nativity sets, I did what I did without any special messages from God. God sent me no angel choir. God did not alert me to a particularly bright star in the night sky. God gave me no dreams, no visions, and no divine visitors. I got no inside information whatsoever to cue me in to the holy significance of that knock on my door from that disheveled couple with their urgent request.

Under what circumstances would a hotel manager in your day book a room for a woman who is nine-months-pregnant to deliver her baby on the premises? How would the other guests feel listening to all that racket for twelve hours? Sixteen? Twenty hours or more? (Kindly remember, in the days of Caesar Augustus, there were no epidurals.) Then there'd be the clean-up—the blood, the afterbirth, and heaps of laundry. Plus there's the problem of what to do with the new mother and her squalling newborn the next day, and the next day after that.

I've been called every name in the book for the decision I made, but the facts are: I came up with a workable plan. I gave what I had.

Kindly remember, I did not know then what you know now. I did not know who was about to be born, or that it was Christmas night. I had no idea. If Joseph was "of the house and lineage of David," no one told me (Luke 2:4, NKJV). Besides, where were Joseph's relatives? Why didn't they open their homes to one of their own? Kinship ties were strong in my culture, so don't blame me if I wondered why this couple had no decent place to give birth and literally no willing helpers. If their own relatives offered no assistance, where was the logic for me to offer mine?

Maybe logic wasn't the driving factor for me that night at all. Inn-keeping was my trade, but hospitality—broadly speaking—was a core value in my culture and a virtue in my faith tradition. The scriptures revere Abraham and Sarah for entertaining angels unawares. Like all Jewish children, I was taught from an early age to welcome strangers, immigrants, and outcasts. When I grew up, I went into the hospitality business. I had my reasons. Do my reasons matter?

Maybe I made hospitality my business because I was good at it. Maybe I did it because I enjoyed it and because the duties fit so beautifully with my religious faith. Maybe innkeeping was both my gift and my calling.

Maybe I'm what you call a people person, the sort who's the first to arrive and last to leave at every party. Maybe I have what you call the gift of gab. Maybe I took to the hospitality business like a fish to water. Maybe I thanked God every day that I could get paid to do what I would have wanted to do anyway: shelter travelers, offer comfortable lodging, and ensure strangers a night or two of safety in a dangerous world.

Or maybe not. Maybe I wasn't suited to this work at all. Maybe I had zero choice in the matter of my profession. In my culture, in our economy under Roman occupation, options were limited. Nobody told us to follow our bliss or find our passion or manifest our heart's desire. If your family was known for something, chances are you'd step into the family business as soon as you were old enough. You'd run errands as a boy. You'd watch your elders and absorb the subtleties of their work without even realizing it. Over time, you'd move into greater and greater responsibilities. Finally, when your elders could no longer keep up, you'd find yourself in charge.

So, maybe I wasn't a natural-born innkeeper by temperament. Maybe I was an introvert. Maybe being around lots of people all the time was exhausting for me. Maybe I was—maybe I *am*—a man of few words, all eyes and ears, utterly mismatched to the only job available to me.

Did I yearn to study Torah and become a rabbi? Did I envy my neighbors in the trades—potters, carpenters, smiths? Maybe I wanted my own plot of land to till and plant and harvest. You don't know, do you?

As for the night itself, it's possible my inn was already full that first Christmas because word had gotten out that I was a decent fellow who wouldn't turn away a weary traveler if he could help it. It's possible someone in town took Joseph aside and pointed him in my direction, saying, "He's known for letting the town drunks crash and sleep it off in his barn. If the inn's full, ask for the barn."

Or maybe my wife was the decent one. Maybe her heart went out to that young couple, wilting with exhaustion, on our doorstep that fateful night. Maybe she mouthed the words, "I'll handle this," then dropped everything to sweep and mop and prepare a pallet on the stable floor. Maybe she stayed on to help with the birth. Or maybe my wife had died years earlier in childbirth. Maybe I paced up and down, worrying myself sick the whole night, until I knew that this mother and baby had made it through. You'll never know.

The reverse could be true as well. Christmas night could have been a one-off for me and my wife. That young couple might have gotten lucky to catch us in a generous mood after one too many wineskins passed between us. Or maybe we knew desperation when we saw it and jumped on the chance to overcharge them.

Who I am is not for you to know. This is not a heart-to-heart. We are not friends. I don't know you, and you don't know me. I am a person, not an inkblot. Beyond that, here is all that can be known about me from the biblical record: I am an essential worker with a private life. I performed a necessary function at Christmastime which was to give that young couple a roof over their heads and a safe enough, warm enough environment to have their baby, the little Lord Jesus. I provided what was needed.

What does Christmas mean to me? This much I can say. I am an innkeeper. Christmas is what I do. People and experiences present themselves. Sometimes they arrive on my doorstep unannounced; sometimes they are expected. I meet eagerly or with dread. Either way,

I open my doors. I find room. I make room. I get creative. I adjust. It is my sacred obligation to welcome whomever God sends as if that person were God's own child, whether I feel like it or not. I offer hospitality; I open my door and with it the door to my heart—at least as far as I am able—to the ones who come. Christmas means doing that.

Thirteen centuries after the birth of Jesus, a Persian poet named Rumi wrote a poem that I like to think I might have written myself if I had a moment's time for poetry (and a little bit of talent). "This being human is a guest house," his poem begins. He depicts ordinary occurrences and disruptions as honored guests, and says, "Welcome and entertain them all."

I'm no poet, and I'm no theologian, and to be honest, but I have one more thing to add. Rumi says, "This being human is a guest house." I say, God is a guest house too, or at least God operates one. In God's guest house, there are a great many rooms. All who care to enter will find a room prepared for them. And not only a room, but also a meal. And not only a meal, but a seat at the table with the Lord Jesus himself presiding.

The way I see it, this "being a guest house" is the heart of the matter. Christmas is God being God and humans being humans. It is us being in one another's company, sharing close quarters.

Warmest wishes,

The Innkeeper

Prayer of Confession

God of divine hospitality, I confess I am unwilling to let just anybody into my life. Forgive me for those times when I act more like a bouncer than an innkeeper, more like a gatekeeper than a gracious host. Help me to maintain a spacious interiority during this busy holiday season. Save me from the folly of closing my door on those you yourself bring to my doorstep. I pray in Christ's name. Amen.

Questions for Reflection

1. Is "Christmas" a verb? How does it change our view of Christmas to think of it as something we do rather than as a date on a calendar?
2. Is Christmas a way of life? What are the central tenets of this way of life? What attitudes does it encourage us to develop?
3. Prior to reading this letter, what impression did you have of the innkeeper in Bethlehem? What characteristics did you assign to him or her? How has this letter changed your impression?
4. In whose home or in whose company do you feel safe, at peace, and unconditionally welcome? What does it mean to you to feel these things in their presence?
5. Will you be welcoming people into your home this holiday season? What insights from the innkeeper's letter do you want to keep in the front of your mind as you prepare to share space, meals, and time with others?
6. In a number of biblical translations, the word "inn" does not appear in Luke 2:7 at all. The original Greek is often translated as "guest room" in these other versions. Does this detail change your understanding of things? How so?

Journaling Prompts

1. How hospitable are you toward yourself? Do you offer safety, peace, and unconditional welcome to all the parts of yourself, or just the parts you are proud of? How might you make yourself more "at home" with your own self?

2. Reflect on any unexpected or unwelcome guests (not necessarily people) who have come to your door and taken up residence in your space. Name these guests. Write out a brief welcome speech to honor each guest and express your gratitude for what they bring. Search out "The Guest House" by Jalaluddin Rumi, and read it for inspiration.

3. The innkeeper makes the point that he played his part in the Christmas story without any direct guidance from God. Have there been times in your life where you've had to make decisions without a clear sense of where God was leading you? Write a short letter back to the innkeeper about one of those times.

Closing Prayer

God, teach me the spiritual art of hospitality. Make an innkeeper out of me. When I am alone and out of sorts, guide my feet to an open door where grace is served and love is the common language. Help me, wherever I am, to create safe spaces for the broken to heal and the weary to find rest. Like the innkeeper of Bethlehem, let me make room and reserve judgment, now and always. Amen.

CHAPTER SEVEN

No Holiday
A Letter from the Midwife

Psalm 22:9-10, Romans 8:22-23

DEAR SISTERS AND BROTHERS,

What does Christmas mean to me? Who wants to know? I'm not saying that to be snarky; it's just that after all these years—centuries—of being invisible, it comes as a shock for me to be acknowledged and invited into a theological conversation.

Don't think that I haven't noticed my absence—not just from your nativity sets and Christmas pageants—but from the Gospels themselves. No one has any trouble adding an innkeeper to the Christmas story, even though no such person is mentioned in the scriptures. I wonder why I haven't been given an equally well-established role in the divine drama.

Perhaps you lack the imagination to picture a midwife showing up to do what midwives do when it came time for Mary to deliver her child. Surely you realize someone had to have sent for help when

Mary, a first-time mother, went into labor, especially since both she and her husband had more than an inkling that the child being born was no ordinary child.

What does Christmas mean to me? Well, it was no holiday. Let's start there.

When you attend a birth, you arrive knowing you'll stay as long it takes. You show up prepared to do everything in your power to keep both mother and baby alive. You pack accordingly—medicinal herbs, clean cloths, a sharp knife (because a snip is better than a tear), a birthing stool or bricks for her to stand on so you can reach underneath to catch the newborn.

You'll need water too, lots of it. You'll clean when you arrive, and you'll clean as you go. You'll clean again afterward—mother and baby—whether they live or whether they die. You'll want to bring at least one helper for the lifting and fetching and to give you a short break when you can't go on without one.

That's how I spent Christmas, working. That's what I remember—the work.

Placing my hands on her taut belly, skin on skin, pressing down to probe. Where is the head? Will it be breach? Asking if she would allow me to look, or at least feel, between her legs? Explaining that I need to know how wide, that I need to keep checking, for her sake, for the baby's.

Making conversation. Getting her to talk a little, but not too much, between contractions. Not acting surprised about the angel. Nodding my head at the words, "He will be great . . . he will reign . . . he will be holy; he will be called Son of God." Believing her, at least in the moment, knowing she needed that from me. Knowing that if I trusted that what she told me was true, then she would trust me when I told her to squat or walk it out or wait or push, **now.**

Cupping Mary's face in my hands, I told her, "Don't be afraid," knowing how dangerous childbirth was for women in my day, knowing full well that I would either be the one to bring her squalling newborn to her breast or the one to close her eyelids if she bled out.

Girding myself for the pain that would be hers. Guiding her breath so that she would drop her jaw and keep her throat open when the contractions came. Trusting my instincts to interpret her animalistic sounds—a grunt, a moan, a roar. So near was I to her white, hot pain it could have been my own.

Giving myself over to the birthing, as I always did, losing myself, but keeping my wits about me—relying on my experiences, my judgment, my intuitions, my intellect, my strength, and my gentleness. Giving myself entirely to the work before me, this woman, this child, as if I'd been anointed, as if I'd been ordained.

I know my work is holy. I know this to be true even though midwives have no place, no standing, in the formal religious establishment. I know it despite the rules concerning what is holy and what is profane, rules that never seem to tilt in our favor. The law designates women as ritually impure for thirty-three days after giving birth to a boy, and sixty-six days after giving birth to a girl (Leviticus 12:1-5). So, where does that leave us as midwives? We attend births. We handle women's pregnant bodies. We wipe up blood and bodily fluids. We dispose of the afterbirth. We do this day in and day out. Is there no end to our profanity?

Yet the birth of a healthy baby is, by all accounts, a religious experience. Who's to say that my work isn't sacred? Call me a heretic, if you will, but the way I see it, a midwife doesn't represent God any less than prophets, priests, or kings. In fact, one of Israel's ancient hymns celebrates God as our divine midwife!

Yet it was you who took me from the womb;
>   you kept me safe on my mother's breast.
On you I was cast from my birth,
>   and since my mother bore me you have been my God
>   (Psalm 22:9-10).

You asked what Christmas means to me. Trust me, I'm getting there, but first I need to know if there's something else behind your question. I need to know if your question is more about Mary than about me. I have a sneaking suspicion that some of you may be angling for me to medically corroborate those words, "born of the virgin Mary," that you recite in the Apostles' Creed.

Listen, a midwife sees and hears many things during labor that she must keep to herself. All filters are off when the contractions come. We don't take advantage of that. We don't gossip. We just don't.

So please don't look to me for any particulars about Mary's hymen. There, I said it—hymen. Yes, I have information that no one else has. I saw what I saw, but you will have to decide what you believe about her condition—and about the divinity and the humanity of Jesus—without that information. Does your understanding of Christmas rest on that one salacious detail? Mine does not, and that's all I have to say about that.

As for what Christmas means to me, let's begin with the obvious. I delivered the baby, for God's sake! I cupped my hands to receive the child born of Mary. I was the first to see his face, the first to study his tiny naked body. From my mouth came the words, "It's a boy!" I bathed him. I swaddled him. I brought him to Mary's breast.

Midwives remember the babies we deliver. We know all the mothers (and most of the fathers). We keep a close eye on the children in our villages—the ones we helped bring into the world—as if they were, in some sense, our own. We delight in their personalities; we are proud of their accomplishments, and we laugh at their antics. I would've liked to watch Jesus grow, but when Herod ordered the slaughter of every boy under the age of two, the family vanished.

Herod's edict wounded our community deeply; it ripped through us with the ferocity of shrapnel from a cluster bomb. The cry of every mother for her murdered baby boy was the cry of our ancestor, Rachel, weeping for a generation of her children. For years to come, all I could remember of Christmas was the carnage that followed. Every anniversary reopened the wound.

Years later, when my own children were grown and my eyesight was fading, word reached us in Bethlehem of a teacher and healer from Nazareth, up north in Galilee, announcing that the kingdom of God had arrived. *Another Messiah-Wanna-Be*, was my first thought, but I listened to the reports along with everyone else.

"Blessed are the peacemakers, the poor, and the meek," he said. *That's us*, I thought to myself. "Let the children come to me," he said. *Spoken like a true midwife*, I smiled broadly. He broke customs and religious laws to speak with, touch, heal, and defend women from their accusers. *Inconceivable!*

"I delivered a baby named Jesus," I mentioned to my daughter one day. "During labor, his mother went on about an angel, said the boy would be great, the Son of the Most High, and so on. This Jesus seems to be about the right age," I said. "Do you suppose . . . ?"

People followed Jesus in droves, but he also made enemies, enemies in high places. When they crucified him, a dark rage coursed through me, with an intensity I hadn't felt since the slaughter of the innocents. When some women reported seeing him alive again, many scoffed, but I chose to believe. I had no reason not to. As if alert to some cosmic transition, I knelt at the news, cupped my hands, and held them out, open and waiting.

What does Christmas mean to me now? For one thing, it means the church was wrong to exclude women from the priesthood for all those years. My female hands were the first to handle the Word made flesh. And am I not a woman? If I can be trusted to reach my hands inside the mother of the Lord and draw her child into the light, cannot women's hands be entrusted with all manner of sacred things? Was I not the first priest of the Christian era?

Look at your nativity sets! Count how many women you see. I'm guessing there's one. The Gospel story takes us right up to Mary's birth pangs, then pauses, picking up again when the men come back in. But the delivery of Christmas was an entirely female affair. Jesus was born to a woman with the help of women. Match the women of Christmas up with the women of Easter and you'll see there's a pattern.

Do you know the French word for midwife? It's *sage-femme*. *Sage* means wise and *femme* means woman. The funny thing is you have "wise men" in your nativity set, don't you? *Sages-hommes?* Where are the *sages-femme?* Are you intimidated by our wisdom? Disturbed by our female power? God wasn't. God trusted me and my young helper to do our jobs. We took the Incarnation into our hands, and you are the beneficiaries. You're welcome.

I'm not trying to make myself the star of Christmas; I'm not. I'm simply trying to erase my erasure, because without me, you don't have the whole story. Have you heard the saying, "God comes to you disguised as your life"? For me, that is true. I see God in me. Go ahead, laugh. I know how that sounds, but here's what I mean. God is a midwife. The world is a pregnant body, fertile with holiness. You can find God at work wherever this holiness wrestles its way out of confinement. You can join God in the work of labor and delivery.

Christmas—the Incarnation—turns holiness inside out. What was hidden is brought into the light. God is the midwife of all of this. Hold out your hands. That slippery thing called hope, waiting to drop, needs you to be ready.

I'm grateful that you asked for my point of view on this subject. As you can see, I've been very forthright, perhaps too forthright. After so many years of silence, it's hard to know where to start or when to stop. I'll stop here.

Merry Christmas,

The Midwife

Prayer of Confession

Attentive God, I confess that I treat people differently depending on how important they are to me. Show me the infinite value of those I ignore. Bring forth in me a change of heart, so that I might change my ways. This, I pray, in Christ's name. Amen.

Questions for Reflection

1. This letter portrays the midwife as a skilled professional helping God deliver on God's promise at a pivotal moment in salvation history. What is lost by the midwife's absence from the Christmas story as we tell it? Why do you think her imagined voice from the margins merits a chapter of its own in this book?

2. In this letter, the midwife recalls the first Christmas as a workday. Who does our society rely on to work through Christmas Eve and Christmas Day? How might celebrating the

midwife's invisible contributions to God's story direct our attention to others whose hard work tends to be ignored or taken for granted? Make a plan to care for a person or people in your community who will be working through Christmas.

3. Re-read Psalm 22:9-10. How does it feel to address God as midwife? Re-read Romans 8:22-23. What is messy about the notion of a world in labor? What is thrilling? What is dangerous? What can midwifery teach you about discipleship?

4. Some major branches of the Christian tradition hold that Mary did not suffer labor pains when delivering Jesus. The doctrinal basis for this position is that labor pains are a consequence of original sin (Genesis 1:16), therefore Mary's freedom from original sin due to her immaculate conception exempted her. What have you been taught? What do you make of this interpretation?

5. Byzantine icons depicting the nativity of Jesus commonly include a secondary scene featuring two midwives—or a midwife and her helper—bathing the divine child. These bathing scenes do not come from the canonical Gospels but from apocryphal (non-canonical) writings. By the eighteenth and nineteenth centuries, many were painted over. The bare arms of the midwives scandalized certain monks, and the portrayal of ordinary women helping and handling the divine child was felt to besmirch his purity. Why do you think icon painters originally depicted this scene? What do you think about the reasons for painting over them? How does this knowledge affect the way you read the letter from the midwife?

Journaling Prompts

1. Reflect on the French word for midwife, *sage-femme*. The punchline of a very old joke says that if the magi were women, they would have asked for directions, arrived on time, helped deliver the baby, cleaned the stable, made a casserole, and brought practical gifts. Read Matthew 2:1-12 (the story of the wise men), and then write a story of equal length featuring the midwives as *sages-femme*.

2. Search for the Advent poem, "If You Want" by St. John of the Cross and translated by Daniel Ladinsky. Reflect on the line, "For each of us is the midwife of God, each of us." Who or what comes to mind? Finish the sentence, "I am a midwife of God when I . . ."

   Reflect on the line, "If you want, the virgin will come walking down the street . . ." Ask yourself, "What is it that I want?" Write what you want.

Closing Prayer

God, our midwife, show me where your holiness is wrestling its way out of confinement and put me to work alongside you in those places. Let me assist in the labor and delivery. Put what is new in my arms to guard and to nurture for the life of the world. Be born in me—be born in us—today. Amen.

CHAPTER EIGHT

Nobody Important
A Letter from a Shepherd

Luke 2:8-20

DEAR WHOEVER-YOU-ARE,

It's kinda weird, you getting a letter from me, don'tcha think? Kinda weird you asking for my thoughts about such an important topic as Christmas, me being a shepherd and all, dirt poor. I'm the kinda guy who's gone all hours of the day and night working a job you'd never want in a million years. I'm the kinda guy you wouldn't want your daughter to marry, smelling the way I do, like sheep and grass and animal dung and God knows what else.

Is it really me you're interested in? Lots of people like the idea of me. They like how I appear in Christmas pageants, especially if it's their own cute kid in a bathrobe holding a stuffed sheep and pretending to be me. But who honestly likes the reality of me? I'm a borderline scoundrel; I'm low class. We know you wouldn't let your cute kid anywhere near me in real life.

I almost said no to the letter. See, my kind don't appreciate y'all trotting us out to give "the poor person's perspective" on things, as if I could speak for every poor person that ever lived, as if I'd want to. I don't wanna end up in your book out of pity.

Plus, it's kinda weird you asking me to write a letter at all, don'tcha think, considering as I'm illiterate. What? The thought never occurred to you? Not one of you said, "Hold on a sec, can the guy even write?" I'm guessing no.

I was gonna say thanks, but no thanks, then I changed my mind. Found me a scribe to do the writing part. Figured I had something to say and nothing to lose. Might as well try.

What Christmas means to me, numero uno, is that God doesn't ignore us poor people the way everyone else does. I'm not saying God pities us; I'm saying God is one of us. Jesus got himself born in conditions about as miserable as you can think of. Then God's messengers announced his birth to nobody but me and my guys. Think about that.

It was just me and my guys out there in the pitch dark on Christmas night when the angels came swooping in. Scared the bejeezus out of us, they did! Nobody "important" was there with us to back up our story afterward. No big shots were around who could swear on a stack of Torah scrolls that yes, there were angels, and yes, there was singing, and yes, one of 'em said, "the Messiah, the Lord" (Luke 2:11). It was just us. No priests, no rabbis, no merchants, no lawyers.

Kinda weird, don'tcha think? We were a rough bunch, me and my guys. Our hill country was like your wild west, I guess. Stuff happened. We did what we had to do for the money, which wasn't great. We left our wives and kids at home, unprotected, sometimes for weeks on end. There was no way to avoid that, but it raised a lot of eyebrows. Irresponsible, they called us, and unreliable.

But then Christmas happened, and it was just us clowns out there when it all went down. Just thinking about it makes me laugh. I can't stop. I just laugh and laugh and laugh 'til I about split my gut.

You hear Mary's song? "He has scattered the proud in the imagination of their hearts. He has brought down the powerful from their thrones and he lifted up the lowly" (Luke 1:51-52). Mary was right. That's what Christmas did—it lifted us up. We were the "lowly" is what I'm saying.

Jesus was born poor, and one thing we noticed was, being poor didn't embarrass him, even when he got famous later on. We loved him for that. "The Spirit of the Lord is upon me, because he has anointed me to bring good news to the poor," he'd say when he got going with his teaching (Luke 4:18). The rich people in the crowds would snarl, but we would grin, pump our fists, and egg him on.

When we could get away with it, we'd listen to him all day. Then we'd stay up half the night smoking our pipes, shivering in the damp air, going back over the whole thing—what he said, how he said it, the reactions he got. It killed us the way he got on rich people's nerves, like he wanted to or something. And the way he made us poor folk feel, man, it was like we mattered.

I'm making a big deal about Jesus being poor and us being poor 'cause being poor is a big deal, a big freakin' deal. If you've never been poor yourself, then you won't understand—scraping by on next to nothing month after month, sending your own kids to bed hungry, then burning hot with shame all night for having done so. For us poor folks to hang around Jesus and hear him speak the way he did—it gave us, I don't know, dignity. Do you know what it's like to live without dignity? We do.

Seems like Jesus was always talking about money, and I gotta hand it to him, the guy had guts. He'd see some hot shot in the crowd, corrupt as all get out, and he'd lock eyes with the guy and launch into one of his parables. "The Widow's Mite," God I love that one! Or "The Rich Man and Lazarus," that's another one of my favorites. To the fat cats, he preached about greed; to the hypocrites, he preached about self-righteousness. Then, when he'd wrap up for the day, we'd wave him over, thump him on the back, shoot the breeze, mess around, crack jokes, and reach in our packs to scrounge up whatever food we had on us to share—bread, olives, maybe some figs.

Whoever else Jesus was—God, the Messiah, whatever—we knew he was one of us. He hung out with us whenever he could, by choice. No wonder those angels came to us and no one else the night he was born. Kinda makes sense in a weird way, don'tcha think?

That brings me to the second thing I want to say in this letter, the second thing that Christmas means to me: responsibility.

Me and my guys, we heard the angels on Christmas night. We listened. We sprinted into town, found the stable, and saw the child sleeping in the manger with our own two eyes; we saw him there, all red and wrinkled, surrounded by chickens and goats. He could've been one of our babies, that's how poor he was—and how magnificent.

We stuck around, we stared, we shifted from one foot to another, we rubbed our hands together and blew on them to stay warm. We were waiting to see who else would show up. We figured the angels had been rushing around telling the whole world. We expected a crowd, but no, nobody came. It was just me and my guys. Go figure.

I studied that baby 'til I memorized him. The Savior, the Messiah, the Lord, that's what the angel called him. I looked from him to us, from us to him and just shook my head. I felt dizzy, then sick to my stomach. A golden silence seemed to muffle all sound, and I felt this crushing weight press down on me from above—as if God had hoisted a hundred-pound sack of grain on my back and anointed my head with oil, all at once. That's when I knew that what I'd been looking at wasn't for my eyes alone. What me and my guys heard that night in the fields wasn't for our ears only. If we said nothing, no one would know.

But if we talked, who would believe us? My mind raced. If one of those big cedar trees falls to the forest floor in Lebanon with no one there to hear it, does it make a sound? If an angel appears to a bunch of poor shepherds with a divine message, and those shepherds fail to tell a single other human soul, would that message get through? Duh, no, obviously not! But why would God give such important information to a no-name like me? Who would take my word for something so . . . earth-shattering?

I looked at the baby some more. A gray dove above me flapped its wings, cooed, then resettled to roost. A mother goat bleated for her kid, and still the boy slept on. I couldn't take my eyes off him until they blurred with tears. Then I was trembling, shaking all over, my staff clattered to the floor, my legs gave out, and I fell to my knees for another birth, mine. There in the cold, in the damp, in the dark, God made something more out of me than a scoundrel and a shepherd. He delivered me is what I'm saying.

From that night on, me and my guys, we were never the same. We'd been brutes and clowns when we came to the manger. We left as a band of heavenly messengers; angels, I guess you could say. God poured out the glory of Christmas on us. God made Christmas our responsibility.

We did what we had to do. We went back to our flocks and fields, then back to our homes and villages, "glorifying and praising God" for all we "had heard and seen as it had been told" to us (Luke 2:20). We about drove our wives mad talking about Christmas and nothing but Christmas 'til we were blue in the face.

Just think what could've happened if me and my guys had kept our mouths shut. Would you—or anybody else—know that Jesus is called Savior, Messiah and Lord? Would you know that his birth was good news of great joy for *all* people or that he came *in* peace to bring peace? Would you know to not be afraid? Would you—or anybody else—know how much Jesus, God in the flesh, respects and trusts poor people, people who—half the time—nobody bothers to respect or trust at all.

So, don't you be keeping your mouths shut either is what I'm saying. Whoever you are, whoever you aren't, don't think for a minute that you and your choices don't matter to God. Your voice counts for something. You gotta believe me on this, and you gotta get yourself ready for whatever job God throws your way. Then, do what you have to do, even if you think you're the least qualified person in the world for the task, even if they call you unreliable or irresponsible or worse. Say what you have to say, even if you're sure no one will listen.

Take me, for example. I never thought anyone would listen to me, but here are you are, listening.

Thank you for that. Merry Christmas!

Yours truly,

A shepherd

Prayer of Confession

God, forgive me when I get sentimental about the Christmas story. Correct me when I turn the poverty of Christ's birth into a scene of softly-lit serenity. Have mercy on me when I tell myself that the grinding poverty of the world's poor simply can't be helped. Forgive me and send me into the fray. I pray in Christ's name. Amen.

Questions for Reflection

1. The title given to the shepherd's letter is "Nobody Important." What does this title mean to you? What themes does it highlight? What questions does it raise?

2. The shepherd addresses his letter to "Dear Whoever-You-Are." What do you think is meant by this choice of words?

3. Food pantries and charitable organizations generally see an increase in donations during the Christmas season. What might the shepherd who wrote this letter have to say about that? Why?

Journaling Prompts

1. Reflect on the shepherd's statement, "I'm saying God is one of us." Listen to a recording of Joan Osborne singing, "One of Us." Pay particular attention to the chorus, which includes the lines, "What if God was one of us? / Just a slob like one of us." What thoughts or feelings does this song bring to mind? How do you think they connect to this letter?

2. In this letter, the shepherd says, "I don't wanna end up in your book out of pity." Write about a time when you felt that you were the object of pity or charity. Then, ask yourself whom you may have treated as an object of pity or charity. What changes would you like to make in yourself?

3. In this letter, the shepherd asks, "Do you know what it's like to live without dignity?" He follows up with a terse, two-word sentence, "We do." In your journal, write your response to the shepherd's provocative question.

Closing Prayer

God of the poor, from the poverty of my heart, let your love bring forth streams of generosity. Make me rich in what matters to you. In all else, I ask only that you give me my daily bread. In Christ, Amen.

CHAPTER NINE

Christmas Casualties
A Letter from Joseph

Matthew 1:18-25,
Matthew 2:13-15, 19-23

A LETTER TO THE CURIOUS,

You've been wondering about me for years, haven't you? You know that I'm Mary's husband. You know I'm Jesus' father, sort of. The Bible quotes me exactly zero times, so while you may think about me off and on, I don't generally stay in the forefront of anyone's mind for very long.

Quiet people like me are used to this. Wood is my medium, not language. Ask me to do something, I'll do it. Ask me to build something, I'll build it. But public speaking? Letter writing? Not my thing.

You ask what Christmas means to me, and my first thought is, are you kidding? Isn't it obvious? Look at my actions. Haven't I already answered that question as clearly as I can? Quiet people the world over will never understand why we are constantly being asked to explain ourselves with words when our actions have already spoken volumes. But if you're still wondering, then here goes. I'll do my best.

For me, Christmas was the end of everything I knew for certain. If I could choose to add a new Christmas carol to your hymnals, it would be the REM song, "It's the End of the World as We Know It (And I Feel Fine)." Christmas was a colossal disruption. It marked the end of my quiet life as a devout Jew doing what devout Jews were expected to do. That wasn't a bad thing, but it wasn't exactly easy. There were casualties.

The first casualty was my faith. Yes, my faith. I was engaged to Mary, which in my day amounted to a legally binding contract. I planned to take Mary as my wife, provided we both lived chastely under that obligation until our wedding day. Then, I discovered she was pregnant. Of course, I thought the only possible explanation for her pregnancy was infidelity, for which my Jewish faith gave me two choices. I could make a public accusation against Mary, knowing she would likely be stoned to death for it, or I could divorce Mary and dissolve our engagement quietly. The first choice would have upheld my honor in the eyes of the community, but I chose the second. It seemed the kinder of the two options available to me.

No sooner did I make up my mind than God asked me to unmake it. A messenger from God spoke to me in a dream and goaded me to do what a decent Jew must not. The messenger told me to stay with Mary in her condition. In other words, break faith with my faith and go through with the wedding, consequences be damned. "The child conceived in her is from the Holy Spirit," was the explanation . . . which explained nothing (Matthew 1:20).

I'm a descendant of the great King David. Mary is not. At some point in our lives, all the men on my side of the family secretly wonder whether their first-born son would be the one to reclaim the throne of David. The messenger in my dream led me to believe the child in

Mary's womb was the one we'd all been waiting for. But how? It made no sense. The Messiah, we all understood, would be from the house and lineage of David. How could Mary's baby be from that house and that lineage when he wasn't, in fact, my son? How could the prophecy be fulfilled on such a tenuous basis?

To make matters more confusing, the messenger in my dream told me what to name the child and told me to do the naming as if I were the child's father! "You are to name him Jesus," the angel said, which means, "God saves" (Matthew 1:21). If I consented to this cockamamie scheme, either I would be a mockery of a father ("not the real father," people would say), or my son would be the laughingstock of his peers ("little bastard thinks he's the Messiah").

In all these ways, the messenger asked me to trust God directly and dismiss what I had been taught to believe by people I respected. The choice was a terrible one. A man, I'd been taught, should not love a woman more than he loves God. This seemed to be what my dream demanded from me. How could I trust such a dream? Why would I trust a mere dream more than the teachings of the rabbis and priests I'd known since childhood?

What Christmas means to me, first and foremost, is this great disruption to my faith. I said yes to God and no to my idea of God. Yes, to my dream, and no to my culture. I said yes to the child in my fiancée's belly and yes to thinking things through for myself even though I am only a carpenter and not an educated rabbi. I said yes to what could have been a figment of my imagination, and I said no to a life without Mary and the baby growing in her womb.

Faith, as I'd known, it was the first casualty of Christmas. The second was my home.

I had a home in Galilee. When I left for Bethlehem with Mary to register for the census (which is a nice way of saying "to pay our taxes"), I expected to return home. Then, Jesus was born, and before we could get back to Galilee, King Herod flew into a rage, threatening to kill every baby boy in his territory.

That's when I had my next dream. "Get up, take the child and his mother, and flee to Egypt, and remain there until I tell you," God's messenger said (Matthew 2:13). "Egypt?" was all Mary could say when I told her the next morning. Egypt was the land of the pharaohs, the land that had enslaved our ancestors. It was the land of foreign gods and graven images, pyramids and taskmasters, plagues and pleadings. We had no money for such a long journey. We had no people in Egypt to take us in. "Herod is about to search for the child, to destroy him," the messenger warned (Matthew 2:13). Was it just a dream, or was it God speaking again?

Could Mary's baby, our baby, be the one Herod was after? Yes, absolutely, and that meant it was time for frantic packing and preparing. We slipped out under cover of darkness, stopping for Mary to nurse, praying the baby won't cry at the wrong time, and then stopping again, praying that Herod's henchmen wouldn't give us a second look at the many checkpoints along the Roman roads.

What Christmas means to me is being displaced, first from Galilee, then from Judea. It means gambling on Egypt, of all the godforsaken places for a Jewish family in the ancient world. It means scrambling for food, water, money, and shelter. It means living as strangers in a strange land for God knows how long. It means two perpetually bewildered parents caring for the Messiah in diapers.

You in the modern world are used to moving every time you get a new job. Your kids move out after they are grown and live in cities halfway across the continent. We did not do this. We were a people rooted in a sense of place. Mary and I were strangers in Egypt. My son's earliest days were lived on the religious, political, and economic margins of an utterly foreign culture. We experienced homelessness, immigration, hostility, and oppression. Ours was a fragile existence.

In the year King Herod died, I had my third dream which triggered our third displacement. This time it was, "Get up, take the child and his mother, and go to the land of Israel, for those who were seeking the child's life are dead" (Matthew 2:20). So, there was even more traveling the perilous Roman roads and another round of starting over again. In Nazareth, we received a polite but distant welcome, our reputation in tatters.

In addition to my faith and my home, the third casualty from Christmas was what I'll call the perks of fatherhood. Like every man in my culture, I wanted a son to carry on the family business. I wanted a son to care for me and my wife in our old age and to prioritize our needs according to the fifth commandment: "Honor your father and mother . . ." (Exodus 20:12). These weren't just hopes and dreams; they were expectations.

Forgive me for wanting and expecting all that from Jesus. The third disruption of Christmas was not getting that sort of son. Jesus did not stay by my side as a carpenter when he grew up. He took off with his friends, called them his disciples, and traipsed around from village to village, preaching, teaching, and performing miracles. Jesus did not make provisions to care for Mary and me in our old age. As for the fifth commandment, I won't say that he dishonored me, but he was far more interested in honoring God. He called God "Father" and "Abba." We didn't see him much once he got going with that preaching business.

But the truth is, I don't mind. I'm not unhappy about any of it. It was the right choice to take Mary as my wife and Jesus as my child. It was the right choice for us to live as refugees in Egypt, and it was right for us to return when we did. What I heard in my dreams was not crazy talk, and I wasn't crazy for listening.

In exchange for the perks of fatherhood, I received a far greater reward. I watched my son take on his work as God's Son. I didn't try to stop him. Not when he left to be baptized by John, not ever. I heard tales of his wonders. I was proud of him. Jesus got everybody thinking for themselves much the way God had demanded that I think for myself years earlier when I'd learned Mary was pregnant. Jesus got everybody to sort through what they'd been taught and compare it with what God actually wants. He got them to weigh things carefully, and make bold choices.

I would have liked him by my side at the carpenter's bench, but I am honored beyond measure to have had a hand in raising him, protecting him, and preparing him for adulthood. I would have liked him to care for Mary and me in our later years, but he died young. He was executed.

Stripped. Flogged. Shamed. Murdered. Don't ask me for details. I won't speak of it. Not to you. Not to anyone.

Then, Easter happened. I don't have words for Easter either. What I can say is that, after all was said and done, Jesus did provide for us in our old age. From Christmas to Easter and beyond, he left us with far more than any father on this earth could ever have asked for or imagined from his son.

I love Christmas. Christmas gave me Jesus for a child, to raise and call my own, and then to relinquish for reasons I will never fully understand. Christmas upended all my expectations for a quietly predictable life. It disturbed me to think for myself. It triggered upheaval and change.

Christmas snatched away the mundane and exchanged it for the wonderful. It deprived me of what I thought I was signing up for when I got engaged to Mary, and it kept me guessing. It caused me plenty of trouble, worry, and sleepless nights. It brought me joy and wonder, but also grief. It made a father out of me, sort of, but truly. It also made me a disciple.

I didn't understand Christmas while it was happening—I still don't—but I was part of it. I didn't know half of what God was doing while God was doing it, but I did the parts God asked me to do.

I hope you are as disturbed by Christmas as I was. I hope it's the end of the world as you knew it, and I hope that, like me, you are fine with that.

I'll end this letter here. I've said more in these few pages than anyone's ever heard me say in one sitting. Words aren't my thing. Anybody can talk. It's what you do that counts.

Truly Yours,

Joseph, son of David

Prayer of Confession

God from whom all the blessings of Christmas flow, I confess that I do not want all of them. I like my life as it is, for the most part. I'm comfortable believing what I believe and not believing what I don't. I'm not looking for you to change any of that. We both know that is a ridiculous attitude on my part. In your mercy, forgive my bullheaded-ness. Change my heart so I may receive with thanksgiving all that you send my way. I pray in Christ's name. Amen.

Questions for Reflection

1. How was Christmas the end of the world as Joseph knew it? What was good and what was bad about that?

2. How do you suppose Joseph's religious upbringing prepared him for the role given to him by God? How might his religious upbringing have been an obstacle for him? Do you view your own religious experiences as a help or a hindrance to your spiritual life today?

3. One way that Joseph describes the impact of Christmas is in terms of casualties. What have you lost by saying "yes" when called by God to do certain tasks? What have you gained? Be specific.

4. Has there been a time in your life when you made a bold choice based on what you believed God was telling you at the time more than on what you'd been taught to believe? What was that like for you? What were the consequences?

Journaling Prompts

1. In this letter, Joseph says, "We were a people rooted in a sense of place." He goes on to describe the impact of being displaced multiple times. What is your experience of place? What is your experience of displacement? Do you have a happy place? Do you have a holy place?

2. In this letter, Joseph acknowledges that being a father to Jesus did not conform to his expectations. What parts of your life now would come as a great surprise to your younger self? How did God shape your story? Write a thank-you letter to your younger self for the great job you did preparing for the unexpected.

3. Joseph accepts the role of raising Jesus although he is not Jesus' biological father. Who besides your parents raised you? Who besides your own children have you nurtured? After

reflecting on these people in your journal, write all their names on little pieces of colored paper and hang them on your Christmas tree.

Closing Prayer

God, I don't like to be interrupted, but I welcome you to interrupt me anytime, anywhere. I don't like it when my plans go awry, but, when I align my will with your will and my spirit with your spirit, I expect that to happen more often. Give me ears to hear your voice and give me sound judgment when I'm called upon to make hard choices. Teach me to think for myself so that I may serve you best throughout all my years. Amen.

CHAPTER TEN

Bring It
A Letter from Mary

Luke 1:26-38, 2:1-10,
and Matthew 2:1-15

DEAR REVELERS,

If roller coasters had been invented when I was a young girl, I would've been first in line. I would've been the one sprinting for a seat in the front car when the ticket takers unhooked the chain to allow for boarding. Once we'd chugged upward and crested the pinnacle of the track, I would've been that daredevil, taking both hands off the grip bars and waving them over my head and shrieking with delight as we picked up speed and my stomach dropped into my pelvis. *Woosh!*

My part of the Christmas story begins with an angel showing up and saying, "Hey Mary, here's an idea. How about getting yourself pregnant outside of marriage? Don't worry, this is God's idea. You'll just need to disregard everything you've ever been taught about *not* getting pregnant outside of marriage, and you'll need to flat out ignore everything ever written in the Torah on the subject, but I promise, you won't regret it. Yes, I do realize you only met me five minutes ago, but I need you to trust me on this. Oh, and did I mention that it's God who will get you pregnant? You lucky girl."

After guarding my virginity as fiercely as a girl my age was expected to, I should have given the angel a firm "No" on the spot. You know, stranger danger and all that. To do otherwise would be the ruin of any young woman, but especially me, dirt poor with zero connections to people in high places. But I said yes. And with that, the angel unlatched the chain and personally ushered me to a seat in the front car of the wild ride that would be the rest of my life.

Actually, I didn't say "Yes" to the angel. My exact words were, "Here am I, the servant of the Lord," and I want to make sure you see what I did there (Luke 1:38). "Here am I" is what important men in the scriptures always say when God gives them important work to do. What a thrill to hear those words coming out of my own mouth, the mouth of a woman! I was Moses in the wilderness startled by a burning bush! I was young Samuel, sleepless after three dreams in a row where God called him by name. I was Isaiah in the Holy of Holies with seraphs winging about overhead, bringing burning hot coals to my lips!

Really, I was just me being me, just Mary, bolted to the ground in the wonder of the present moment. Remember, I was engaged to Joseph and therefore honor-bound to save myself for him. Somehow, I had the nerve to consent on the spot to this new plan of having God's baby. "Here am I," I announced confidently, becoming at that moment the first woman in scripture ever to talk to God in that manner, using those exact words. "Here am I," I said, taking my hands off the grip rails of my obscure life in the permanent underclass of my gender so that I could yield to God as no woman had ever done before in human history. "Let it be with me according to your word" (Luke 1:38). *Woosh!*

Everything about Christmas was a wild ride, and I'd like you to remember it that way. When Joseph found out I was pregnant, he married me anyway. Thank God! I don't know where I would have gone or what I would have done otherwise. Society offered so few options to an unwed mother and all of them were bad. Try not to think about that too much.

Soon after—speaking of wild rides—he and I zig-zagged our way from Nazareth through the hill country of Judea to Bethlehem in a manner I would wish on no pregnant woman anywhere ever. When we discovered there was no room at any of the inns in Bethlehem, I got even more practice in a skill I would use for the rest of my life: making alternate plans on a moment's notice. I was the original Elastigirl. Flexibility was my spiritual gift. My stomach was by no means the only part of me obliged to stretch and accommodate what God had in store.

Standing just inside the stable door with Joseph worrying at my side, I took in its warmth—the mounds of soft hay, the unmistakable smell of animal dung and chicken feathers, the funny sideways chewing of goats. My eyes lingered on the feeding trough. I studied it from several angles, then shrugged, and nodded to Joseph. "Sure, why not?" I said, laughing despite myself. Could things get any stranger than they already were?

When my water broke, my heart soared. But based on what came next, I do not recommend childbirth in a stable. "He will be great," I chanted over and over, repeating the angel's words while swiping at flies between contractions. "Son of the Most High," I heaved, "Throne of David, Son of God, holy" (Luke 1:32). During the worst of the pain, I may or may not have lost my cool. I may or may not have roared from the birthing stool, "God, if this baby is as important as you say he is, why are we doing this the hardest possible way?"

When the baby at last dropped from my womb into the waiting hands of the midwife, we both drew in our breath—as every midwife and every mother has done from time immemorial—and we waited. The next few seconds would be crucial. First, the silence, then, into the interminable void, a celestial squall—the first out-breath of the divine child, a word spoken in the common language of the newly born. What does Christmas mean to me? It means that sound.

I know who my child became. I know what he accomplished and what God accomplished through him. I know all the things that transpired beforehand in anticipation of his birth—all of it recorded in sacred scripture. Based on all of that, here is how I view Christmas: God, having called and sent various people on missions of mercy over the eons, in the fullness of time, looked out over humankind with a new mission in mind and wondered, "Whom shall I send this time?" God pondered the question and arrived at the only possible answer given the enormity of the task. "I will go," God said, "I send me."

On Christmas night in Bethlehem, when Jesus took his first breath and squalled as newborns do, his plaintive cry was none other than the voice of Yahweh, the God of yesterday, today, and forever, announcing, "Here am *I*." The God who does the sending had sent himself.

Hearing the sharp staccato sounds of Jesus' cry, Joseph stopped his pacing and fell to his knees in prayer. The midwife smiled with relief and cut the cord. I reached for my newborn miracle and held his cheek to mine. Now that my labor had ended, the animals adjusted themselves, remaking their beds, and settled in to sleep. But, for me, there was still more to come, more of the never-ending strangeness of Christmas.

I'd barely gotten myself and Jesus bathed and comfortable when shepherd ruffians burst in on us talking about angels. *Angels?* Joseph and I exchanged a knowing glance, and he invited them in. Exhaustion notwithstanding, anyone who'd had a mystical experience as strange, compelling, and assuredly real as ours would be welcome company. Reaching into their sacks, they drew out bread and cheese for an impromptu party. We shared our angel stories and compared the details. One wrinkled fellow with cloudy eyes and leathered skin took a flute from his bag, and the singing began. Soon after, one of them sprang to his feet, followed by another. Their dancing shook the rafters and made me laugh. I fell asleep to the thumping and stomping. When I awoke in morning's light to bring my child to the breast, they were gone without a trace.

Days and nights ran together, as they do with a newborn, and before long, we were on the road again. This time, our destination was the Temple in Jerusalem for my purification and for Jesus' dedication. As it turned out, it was also time for more unsolicited attention from total strangers. While Joseph was negotiating for turtledoves in the outer courtyard of the Temple, a frail bearded man hobbled toward us with a woman older than Methuselah not far behind. When they reached us, the man dropped his cane, took Jesus from my arms, and clasped him as if he'd been waiting for just this moment and just this baby for his entire life. He prayed out loud and so did she. He blessed us warmly.

Then he stopped short and looked sharply at me—no, into me—with a look to chill the heart. His face went dark before he spoke again. "This child is destined for the falling and the rising of many in Israel and to be a sign that will be opposed," he said (Luke 2:34). "And a sword will pierce your own soul, too," he added in a hoarse whisper, jabbing his index finger into my sternum (Luke 2:35). That's when I flew into a rage. I told him to mind his own business and snatched my baby back, nearly knocking the old woman over in the process. I made a scene for which I am now truly sorry.

We returned to Bethlehem. More days and nights ran together after that until the day when we opened our door to a third set of complete strangers. Before us stood wealthy travelers, wearing fine robes dusty from a long journey, holding gifts fit for a king. We beckoned them indoors. I held Jesus in my lap. They bowed, presented their gifts, and spoke quietly to Jesus in a language so different from our own that we could not make out a word of it. We learned nothing about these men. I'm sure they told us their names but the sounds were so foreign to us that we could not recall them later. As before, with the band of shepherds, we shared food and drink. We did a lot of smiling. I let them stroke the baby's soft hair and watched them catch their breath as Jesus' tiny hand curled itself around a bony finger. After staying the night nearby, they left in a rush at dawn's light, talking loudly with exaggerated gestures as if that might help us understand their need for haste.

I thought again of the strange man in the Temple courtyard. I did not want to think about him, but I did.

"What next?" I asked Joseph as we stood side by side waving them on their way. I got my answer from him the very next morning: Egypt, the ancestral land of our sworn enemies. Egypt seemed like an odd place to raise a Jewish baby, let alone this baby, but I am nothing if not flexible. Off we went, zig-zagging our way again, this time with a newborn. Our journey involved crossing a desert and proceeded in a manner I would wish on no mother of a newborn, but such was my life of derring-do. I came to admire God for making things difficult.

After a few years in Egypt, we headed back to the relative quiet of Nazareth. Jesus grew, played, laughed, fought, fussed over his food, and scraped his knees in the manner of all boys everywhere. Well, that's not exactly true. Joseph and I searched for words to describe this feeling we had of living in two intertwined realities. One moment, Jesus startled us with a wisdom beyond his years or a kindness far exceeding that of his friends. In another moment, he exasperated us altogether, as any boy might do. To be the mother of this strange but fascinating puzzle of a child was all trial and error. Our quiet years unspooled from God's hand with all the contradictions of that first Christmas: intensely holy, unbearably mundane.

When Jesus was very young, we would play "I Spy" on our daily walks to the well for water. His way of noticing the crook of an olive branch or the scuttle of a dung beetle awakened something in me, something more than childlike wonder. At home, I took long breaks from my own chores to join him in creative play. Together, we mixed dirt with water for the sun to bake into tiny cakes. We arranged flat stones as banquet tables and laid elaborate feasts for dozens upon dozens of tiny imaginary people. My favorite of all our games was hide and seek. I'd cover my eyes and count slowly to ten while he selected a hiding place. Then I'd search through the house and yard pretending not to see him, all the while edging closer, until he could bear the excitement no longer and burst into view crying, "Here am I!"

With Jesus, every surprise was somehow not surprising. "Now what?" Joseph and I said to each other the day he walked away from carpentry and got himself baptized. "Now what?" we said, when we got wind of his uncanny effect on evil spirits, his healing touch, his harsh words for hypocrites in any guise. "Now what?" we repeated when word reached us of the crowds that swelled and pressed in on him as he traveled from town to town—a mix of savory and unsavory characters, poor and rich, old and young. "Does any of this surprise you?" I remember asking Joseph.

"No . . . and yes," he answered, and that made us both laugh in a worried sort of way.

When we learned of his arrest, I whispered, "What next?" Days and nights ran together. Time sped up, then it slowed way down. Finally, it ground to a catastrophic halt.

After my Jesus breathed his last, with welts on his back and blood weeping from his wounds, I returned home to my husband's crumpled embrace. We wept long and loudly, our bodies convulsed with a pain worse, by far, than the pain of labor. After a long while, I drew back, held his shoulders firmly, looked him in the eyes, and asked, "Are you surprised?"

"No," he answered. "I mean, yes." Then, he gulped for air and exhaled in another spasm of grief while I flew into a rage. "That old man in the Temple was wrong!" I shouted. "This isn't a sword that's piercing me. This is a thousand swords. This isn't my soul in shreds. It's my heart—my son, my beloved."

Jesus' quiet return on Easter morning came as less of a surprise to me than you might imagine. With Christmas as both my reference point and the story of my life, Easter was less of a shock to me and more a heart-rending joy. Our extraordinary child had been given to us from above and placed in my body without fanfare. Now, he had been restored to us from oblivion, also without fanfare. It seemed to me that everything, even the imaginary games we'd played together during his childhood, had been readying us for this very moment. Easter was me glancing up. It was him catching my eye. It was our wordless greeting, one to the other, announcing, "Here am I."

"Are you surprised?" Joseph asked me when I arrived home breathless with the news.

I nodded my head, yes, then shook my head, no, then nodded my head again. Yes.

"He will be great." The old words echoed in my memory—"Son of the Most High. Throne of David. Holy."

If I could do it all again, I would. But I'd make one change. I'd throw a party at the end of every day that Joseph and I spent with Jesus—every single day. I'd fling open our door and call for neighbors and strangers alike to come eat bread and cakes, drink wine and ale, and dance and sing in the presence of such a one as he.

So, I am delighted, twenty-first century Christians, I am beyond delighted to see what a big, huge deal you have made of Christmas. I say, go ahead, deck the halls, in Jesus' name! The more sparkle the better! Let carols ring! (And yes, you can start singing them before Thanksgiving. Why not?) Make and serve delicious food. Throw parties. Fill your homes with strangers. That child of mine attracted the oddest assortment of people to him from day one, so the more the better, I say. Give Christmas all you've got!

That is to say, give Christmas your full consent. Allow the God who came at Christmas to come to you, delight you, and meddle with your life. That's what I did, and look what became of me. I've had my turn. Now it's yours.

Right this way. Why not take the front car?

Buckle up. Hands up. *Woosh*!

Joyfully yours,

Mary

Prayer of Confession

God of Christmas, I confess that I often think of the religious life as a duty and not an adventure. Forgive me for planning my own life instead of leaning forward with curiosity to discover what you have in mind. Forgive my family-comes-first attitude and teach me to leave an open door and a seat at my table in the spirit of Jesus, who makes strangers friends. Amen.

Questions for Reflection

1. Describe Mary's personality and character traits as portrayed in this letter. Compare this portrait of Mary with the way she appears in Christmas cards, nativity pageants, and Christian art. Have you ever thought of Mary as a fun-loving adventurer? Can you picture her lying on her belly playing in the mud with Jesus? Can you picture her tilting her head back and snorting with laughter? Why or why not?

2. Is Christmas a "family holiday"? What do we mean by that? The only people to celebrate Jesus' birth, according to the scriptures, were two different sets of strangers. His ministry brought strangers of all kinds together in new ways, and when he died on the cross, it was between two strangers—common criminals. How might Christmas be more than a "family holiday" this year? To whom might you open your door and invite to your table?

3. Think about the animated film *The Incredibles*. If you haven't seen it, consider watching it. How is Mary like the super-hero mom, Elastigirl? List all the moments in Mary's life that obliged her to stretch, pivot, change plans, and adapt. How do you feel about changing plans on a moment's notice? Is flexibility a spiritual gift? If yes, is it yours?

4. The scandal of pregnancy out of wedlock frequently forced women to provide for themselves and their child through prostitution. Imagine Mary's state of mind—both emotional and spiritual—as she discovered she was pregnant and waited to see whether Joseph would honor their engagement. What thoughts do you think were going through her mind at this time?

5. In this letter Mary says, "I came to admire God for making things difficult." What do you make of this statement? How do you relate to it?

Journaling Prompts

1. For all its joy, Christmas can be a stressful time of year. Rigidity is a common response to stress. Make a list with two columns. In the left-hand column, write what you love about the Christmas season. In the right-hand column, write what you find stressful. Study your lists. What can you cross off the right-hand column? What can you adapt in your right-hand column to make the season less stressful?

2. When things don't go according to plan this Christmas season, what will you do? Brainstorm and write out your intentions. Be specific. Now, go over what you've written and put an asterisk next to the responses you like best. Write each of these on separate pieces of paper and tape them in a prominent place to help you remember.

3. In this letter, Mary think of Jesus' first cry as an announcement of sorts, as if God himself were saying, "Here am I." Do you perceive God to be present here and now? Ask God to help you notice God's presence. Set a timer for three minutes and sit in silent expectation. Then, write what comes to mind; write what you feel, or write a prayer.

4. Write freely for five minutes using the following prompt: *Because of Christmas, Mary . . .*

    Now, write freely for five more minutes using the prompt: *Because of Christmas, I . . .*

Closing Prayer

God, I thank you for making certain things difficult. I give you credit for what you draw out of me despite my shortcomings. I admire you for the gifts I've discovered that I didn't know were mine. Let Mary's life of derring-do give me the courage to run, not walk, into the marvelous unknown of each new day. Show me where to look. Keep me alert and mindful so that I don't miss those moments when you emerge from hiding to make your presence known. Amen.

CHAPTER ELEVEN

Gobsmacked
A Letter from the Wise Men

Matthew 2:1-12

ESTEEMED TWENTY-FIRST-CENTURY CHRISTIANS,

Your request for a letter on the subject "What Christmas means to us" has reached us across both long miles and many centuries. In truth, we chuckled a little at your question because Christmas isn't really our holiday. Our day on the church calendar is Epiphany, January 6, which you in the West virtually ignore.

We know about your Christmas pageants and your live nativities. We know about all those little decorative scenes in your homes with tiny figurines representing shepherds, angels, the Holy Family, and . . . *us*. While we appreciate the attention you lavish on us every year, it seems you remember our story differently than we do.

To begin with, we never saw a single angel, let alone a multitude of heavenly hosts. We heard no celestial choirs. If there were shepherds around, we never ran into them. Our paths simply didn't cross. What puzzles us the most is the way you keep putting us into a stable when you think of us in your mind's eye. Don't you read your own scriptures? We never set foot in a stable. It was "on entering *the house*" that we "saw the child with Mary his mother" (Matthew 2:11).

We weren't there on Christmas night, and we didn't see the baby Jesus lying in a manger. Call us late to the party, if you must, but that chapter of the story was well over by the time we arrived on the scene. We saw him in a house. Maybe you think we're nitpicking over an unimportant detail—stable, house, house, stable, what's the difference? But, if you insist on putting us in that stable on Christmas night along with everyone else, you soften the loneliness of our journey. Everybody loves a happy ending, so it's no wonder you prefer us there in the stable with the whole Christmas gang, dressed in our Christmas outfits, ready for a bow and a curtain call. But there was no Christmas gang, or, if there was, we weren't part of it. What feels like a happy ending to you was only the halfway point for us.

You call us "the wise men," and that's another problem. We made some very unwise choices on our journey to Bethlehem, choices we regret to this day. We are magi; that is, we are Zoroastrian priests from Persia, the country you now call Iran. To be honest, our countrymen do consider us wise and hold us in high regard. We are experts in a skill that your Judeo-Christian scriptures expressly forbid: astrology. We search the night sky for signs and portents that we connect back to the ancient prophet of our religion, Zoroaster, but you might be more familiar with his other name: Zarathustra.

Our legends tell us that Zoroaster was conceived in the womb of a fifteen-year-old Persian virgin,* and that Zoroaster himself predicted "other virgins" would conceive more divinely appointed

* S A. Nigosian, *The Zoroastrian Faith: Tradition and Modern Research* (Montreal, Que.: McGill-Queen's University Press, 1993), 11.

prophets as history unfolded.* So, when we noted the appearance of an unusual star in the night sky, we took it on faith that this star portended just such a birth among the Jewish nation. We were not wrong, were we? We packed our saddle bags and sojourned across the Syrian desert to the land of Judea so we could pay our respects to one who we believed would be as great as our own Zoroaster. Again, we were not wrong, were we?

Where we did go wrong, and horribly so, was in the execution of our plan. We were blundering fools to go to King Herod for information. What were we thinking?! Herod the Great was a tyrant. He ruled by intimidation. Although he was a Jew, his political loyalties were with Rome, and it was Rome who put him on the throne. Since he was not from the house and lineage of King David, he lacked legitimacy in the eyes of the people. The newborn babe would be to Herod what baby Moses had been to Pharaoh in his day, a threat, a usurper.

But in our naiveté, we didn't take all of this into account. We didn't do our homework. We surprised King Herod with the news of the astrological signs announcing a newborn king of the Jews. We had simply assumed that the birth of a new Jewish king would be cause for celebration, but nobody important seemed to know anything about this birth. It was Herod himself who put two and two together. Summoning the chief priests and the scribes, he asked them where *the Messiah* was to be born (Matthew 2:4).

The Messiah! Not just a newborn king, but the Messiah! The God of Israel had promised the Jewish people a Messiah, and devout believers had waited in hope for generations for this Messiah to appear. As soon as Herod made the connection, he suddenly began to show a great deal of interest in the child—too much interest.

---

* Paul Fink, *Comparing and Evaluating the Scriptures* (Lompoc: Summerland Publishing, 2011), 30.

By blundering into his court the way we did, we tipped him off and kindled his jealous rage. It seems our news came as an inconvenient truth. He didn't want the Messiah. The Messiah would be of no use to him. At this particular moment, the Messiah didn't fit into Herod's grand plans. We discovered later that he would rather kill the Messiah than give up one inch of the power and glory he had worked so hard to accumulate. He was Herod the Great, and he wanted to stay that way!

To this day, we tell ourselves that it wasn't our fault. It was Herod's choice to take a page out of Pharaoh's playbook and order the slaughter of all baby boys two years old and under. We tell ourselves that the blood of those children and the tears of their mothers and fathers are on his hands, not ours; on his head, not ours. But we know full well the part we played in the story. We know what our ill-considered assumptions led to, and we carry our anguish with us wherever we go, day in and day out, from one year to the next. The mere sight of a baby brings tears of shame to our eyes. We've each had this experience. Our chests constrict, our hearts race, and we must steady ourselves until grief and regret call off their onslaught.

You asked what Christmas means to us, and the truth is, we can't *not* remember this part of the Christmas story. The birth of Jesus brought on a slaughter of the innocents. Our indiscretions while searching for the child triggered this slaughter. Lord, have mercy on us. Lord, have mercy.

We journeyed on from Herod's palace to Bethlehem where we searched diligently. We canvassed the town until we at last found the child in the aforementioned house with Mary, his mother. As the scriptures accurately report, we were overwhelmed with joy. In his presence, we fell to our knees. We presented our gifts. To say anything more than this will add nothing to the description.

What we saw, what we felt, was nothing less than pure holiness, as if God himself were with us in that bare, cramped house. It was as if we—Zoroastrian priests—had stepped unhindered into the Holy of Holies within the famed Jerusalem Temple! We, Gentile practitioners of the dark arts, had been granted full access. Can you imagine?

Your scriptures call the child Emmanuel, which means "God with us." That is the very name we ourselves would have chosen for him based on our experience, the details of which we simply must leave to your imagination.

Afterward, we wondered, "Where was everybody else?" Christ the Messiah was born, but where were the other dignitaries? Had we really been the only ones to visit? As far as we could tell, there had been no ceremonies, no celebrities, no royal proclamations, no banquets thrown, and no invitations sent. There was no red-carpet treatment, you might say.

Were ours the only gifts given? *Really?*

To be in the presence of the holy child was the most extraordinary moment of our lives. On this, we are in full agreement. We were, and we still are, gobsmacked. We have learned a few things about Judaism since that journey of ours, and if we didn't understand it before, we understand now that people like us, people who do what we do, have no place in Judaism. Divination, sorcery, astrology, augury, practices such as these are an affront to the sovereignty of God.

And yet, it was our "evil" art of astrology that led us to the Christ child. The Jewish Messiah was honored by none other than us—Gentiles who excelled in the very practices expressly prohibited to Jews everywhere. Nothing about this makes sense on paper, yet we know that we belong in the story. The holy child was born for outsiders like us as well as for his own people. *We were his own people.* Despicable though we may be by Jewish standards, there we were nevertheless, kneeling before the Christ child and emptying our treasure chests to offer our gifts. Oh, the wonder!

But, Oh, the loneliness!

We were warned in a dream not to return to Herod, and, at least on this detail, we did not blunder. We kept our information to ourselves, which added to our loneliness. Taking leave of the holy family, we began the long journey home. We trusted no one along the way and, to be honest, no one trusted us. We kept an eye and an ear out for Herod's spies. They were everywhere. We changed our route; we traveled by night, but covering our tracks wasn't easy. Everything about us screamed, "Foreigner!" Everything from our clothes to our mannerisms to our accents to the provisions we carried and the food we ate was liable to attract the attention we so desperately wanted to avoid

Please do not minimize the significance of our predicament. We defied the express instructions of King Herod the Great. In other words, we broke the law. Call it civil disobedience, but we did not do what Herod commanded. Instead, we did what was right in our own eyes, all based on a dream that one of us had.

Had it not been for that dream, chances are we would have gone right back to Herod's palace where we would have blurted out every detail of our experience thereby revealing the location of the child. Chances are we would have played right into Herod's hand. The child would be dead and, most likely, so would we.

You ask what Christmas means to us. We have conferred for a long hours over this question, and here is our answer.

Our experience in your Christmas story—or, more correctly, your Epiphany story—connected us to a God who is larger than any God we thought we knew. You picture us riding camels, searching for the Christ child as if we were on some sort of a quest, but we remember God coming in search of us. Through our expertise in the stars, God got our attention. God beckoned us to act on what we believed the heavens were telling us. God drew us irresistibly toward the place where the child lay.

Our journey from Persia to Bethlehem and back was long and lonely, but God's journey was longer by far. From the highest heavens, God came down to be born in Bethlehem, but in hindsight, we know that God also came down to Persia. God sought us and found us long before we determined to go in search of God.

Ultimately, our role in the divine drama was a cameo. We came. We saw. We left. We don't mind being relegated to this minor role, but we want you to understand its significance: the one born as king of the Jews was not for Jews only. We, the magi, are both evidence of that and witnesses to it. We appear year after year in your manger scenes as scandalous outsiders—party crashers. We believed nothing that your prophets, priests, and kings had taught for centuries. We practiced a religion that was an abomination to your ancestors.

But there we were, and here we still are, year after year—a scandal in your nativity sets, an abomination in your Christmas pageants. O, glorious abomination! For God so loved the world that God did not despise us or our people for our beliefs but instead became known to us *through them!* We may have been blundering fools, but that might be the point. The king of the Jews can also be the king of everybody else, even blundering fools.

Are you a blundering fool? If you are, then step right up. There's room for you here in the holiday tableau, such as it is. You'll fit right in.

Christ was born for you. Christ was born for this. Christ was born to save.

Yours truly,

The Magi from Persia

P.S. Our names are not Melchoir, Casper, and Balthazar. Where did you ever hear that one? You don't need to know our names. You only need to know our story.

Prayer of Confession

Gracious God, we confess that we like to think of ourselves as exemplary Christians. The truth is that we are not. Forgive us for being overly proud of ourselves and overly confident of our own goodness. Help us to learn from those who beheld the newborn Christ child. Change our hearts, so that we may change our ways. Amen.

Questions for Reflection

1. "We were, and we still are, gobsmacked," say the wise men in their letter. Is there a time when you experienced the kind of holy joy described here? Recall the details.
2. In what ways do the wise men fit the profile of unwelcome party-crashers? Whose presence at the manger do you think would have been more suspect in first-century Palestine, the shepherds or the wise men?
3. Popular cultural portrays the wise men as exotic foreigners. What happens to someone's humanity when they are labeled exotic? How might this label have affected your view of the wise men?
4. What is conveyed by the exclamation, "O glorious abomination!" in the above letter? Study the figures of the wise men in your nativity set or as depicted on Christmas cards. Do their depictions adequately convey the strangeness of their role in the story?

Journaling Prompts

1. The wise men made their journey together. Who has shared your search for the divine? With whom did you wander, debate, explore, and discover? Who are your discussion partners now as you continue to reflect and learn?

2. How did you arrive at the manger? Are you still searching? Reflect on your journey. What false starts or errors in judgment have you made? Whose advice did you seek? Was it right or wrong? What draws you to continue seeking the holy?

Prayer

God of all nations, peoples, and cultures, you have made each day bright with your light and your love that is destined for all. Prompt me to look up and notice, then kneel, then offer you my finest gifts. In the radiance of your holy love, let all peoples praise you in their own language and bring you their best. I pray in the name of Jesus. Amen.

CHAPTER TWELVE

One Divine Detail
A Letter from Jesus

Luke 1:46-56,
1 Corinthians 13:1-8

DEAR BELOVED ONE,

This is a love letter. And here is a love poem:

Roses are red, violets are blue.
The meaning of Christmas is, "I love you."

Did I make you laugh? Or at least groan? Good! Now that I have your attention, I want you to know that I'm dead serious. This *is* a love letter—from me to you—written in answer to your question about Christmas.

Given that you're reading this book (and have gotten this far), I don't have to remind you that Christmas is my birthday. The earnest among you have been celebrating for a month with nativity sets on your front lawns and posts about how "Jesus is the reason for the season" on social media. I thank you for that.

But if I were decorating for Christmas, here's what I'd do. I'd rummage through the Valentine's Day bin. I'd string red hearts up everywhere. I'd rip-off that "I heart New York" logo and change it to "I heart you." I'd decorate my Christmas tree with heart-shaped ornaments and nothing else. You'd all get a Valentine's card from me. It'd be homemade, nothing mushy, just the simple truth. I'd put your name in cursive and my name in block letters. Why? Because it's you, my love—well, my loves—who are the reason for the season. Christmas is me loving you.

If you're a churchgoer, you've probably come to expect a yearly sermon from your pastor about putting me first at Christmastime. You'll hear that I'm the real star of Christmas. In opening this letter, I'm guessing you expected more of the same. With all due respect to pastors everywhere, I'm writing to tell you that they've gotten things switched around a bit. Christmas is less about you loving me than it is about me loving you. I hear you sing, "O come, let us adore him," with such joy on Christmas Eve, but I also sing on Christmas Eve. I bend low, I sing you to sleep, and on Christmas morning, I am there to brush the hair from your face, and sing you awake:

I come, for I adore you,
I come, for I adore you,
I come, for I adore you,
my own precious child.

Chances are you've never heard a Sunday sermon admonishing you to put *yourself* first at Christmastime, but that is exactly what I did. I put you first. If I were invited to preach from your pulpit, that would be my message entire. It'd be a one-point sermon, a one-word sermon— you. You are what Christmas means to me. I was born for you. I am

God's gift to you. I dropped from Mary's womb into your life for your joy, your healing, your consolation, and your hope unending.

Even people who don't go to church generally know the salient details of my birth—shepherds, angels, wise men, manger, swaddling clothes. But there is one divine detail that doesn't get nearly enough attention: before I was born, I loved you.

Haven't you noticed my devotion to you all this time? Never mind if you haven't; I'll spell it out for you. My love for you doesn't depend on you noticing. It doesn't depend on you doing anything. Loving you was my choice to make. I have chosen and will keep on choosing you, you, and you, again. My choice holds until the end of time, and if that is how long it takes for you to believe what I am trying to tell you, then so be it. This is a love letter. Christmas is a love story. I was born to love you, and I have done so with every molecule of my being.

If you find this hard to believe, I don't blame you. I know what it is to be you, or rather, to be one of you. I know the deep spiritual damage self-loathing can wreak. I understand your love-hate relationship with love itself. I know how complicated love gets, both the giving and the receiving of it, and I understand how hard it must be to think straight about such important matters when the holiday pressures mount.

I watch you and everyone else go through the paces of Christmas each year with consternation. Much of what you do gladdens my heart, but I'm dismayed to see that the sort of people I prioritized in my ministry have the worst time of it. Year after year after year, those who live from paycheck to paycheck go deeper into debt, the bereaved sink farther into grief, and those who already despise themselves find even more reasons to do so amid the twinkling lights of holiday cheer.

I keep an especially close eye on the children. They are buried under a mountain of advertisements and burdened with a Santa narrative that fuels their material wants. Everyone says Christmas is for children, but I won't believe that until concern for the wellbeing of children extends beyond the annual impulse to buy them things. I'll believe Christmas is for children when you can show me a Macy's trained Jesus in every shopping mall with long lines of little ones eagerly waiting their turn to climb on my lap, hear me call them by name, and tell them that even before they were born I already loved them with an everlasting love.

I find the whole "magic of Christmas" shtick especially tiresome; I urge you to drop it. My love for you is a sacred thing, and my incarnation is one of earth's holiest moments. There's plenty of magic to be found elsewhere. Leave it to the fairy tales, Disney movies, Harry Potter books, and your own imaginations. Build all the pretend worlds you want, worlds where dreams come true and good people get their just rewards, but please leave Christmas out of it. There is no such thing as Christmas magic. None. Zero.

When it comes to Christmas, it's not about magic; it's about truth and wonder and mystery. There is nothing make-believe about divine love. Don't chase fool's gold when the God of yesterday, today, and forever waits at your doorstep.

Here's what I want for Christmas: I want a Christmas overhaul. I want my birthday to celebrate my love for all God's children. I want the holiday with my name on it to bless poor and rich alike. I want it to heal the brokenhearted, mend relationships, change lives, and change the world. I don't want Christmas to *on* your agenda for a few exhausting weeks, then get crossed off, packed into boxes, and stored in your attic until next year. I want Christmas to *be* your agenda. I want Christmas to *set* your agenda for the entire year. Did you hold a toy drive? Excellent, now hold a love drive. Don't know how that would work? Figure it out, my loves. I believe in you.

What I want for Christmas, more than anything, is for you to believe. Let me be more specific. What I want is for you to believe *me*.

Maybe you're a skeptic. Maybe you consider yourself spiritual-but-not-religious. Maybe you have a million and one questions about the historical reality of me that incline you to throw the proverbial baby out with the bath water. I'm not asking you to be someone you are not. Nor am I asking you to believe every single narrative detail about me if you find you cannot. I am asking that you believe the essence of me. I'm inviting you—I am encouraging you—to make a joyful choice and to believe the whole truth of me: I am love, pure, holy, infinite, unchanging, merciful, gracious, slow to anger, powerful beyond measure, made perfect in weakness. All of who I am is aimed squarely at all of who you are, all of the time.

I already told you that this is a love letter and that love letters have love poems, so here is another:

> *Violets are blue, roses are red.*
> *There's only one thing I haven't yet said:*
> *My body was broken, for your sake, I bled.*
> *I died with the weight of the world on my head.*

My Incarnation was all for love's sake, so when you hear the word "Christmas," think "love," and when you hear the word "love," think "Christmas." When you say, "Merry Christmas!" think, "Merry Love!" When you exchange Christmas gifts, call them *love gifts*. Sing love carols. Send love cards. Bake love cookies and roast a love ham. Hang love ornaments on a love tree strung with tiny colored love lights.

You know what? Find 1 Corinthians 13:4-8 in your Bible right now and change it up a just a little. Read it this way: "Christmas is patient; Christmas is kind; Christmas is not envious or boastful or arrogant or rude. Christmas does not insist on its own way; Christmas is not irritable or resentful; Christmas keeps no record of wrongs; Christmas does not rejoice in wrongdoing but rejoices in the truth.

Christmas bears all things, believes all things, hopes all things, endures all things. Christmas never ends."

What does Christmas mean to me? It means I love you, you knucklehead. It means anytime you want to stop chasing the golden ring, the carrot on the stick, the next shiny object that catches your fancy, I, the source and author of you, will be here waiting. Anytime you're ready, I am. I'm not stalking you; I'm no hound of heaven. I'm more like a tree shading you year in and year out whether or not you've noticed.

Christmas is me coming to you with my hand outstretched. Take my hand. That's all I want for Christmas. I cannot be Emmanuel alone. I cannot be who I am apart from you and countless others because my very name means "God-with-us." I wasn't born for my sake. I was born for yours.

Come to me all you who are weary and carrying heavy burdens. Lean on me. Walk with me. I'll bring you to a patch of holy ground, or to a Communion table, or to a mighty river. I'll bring you to a place where even a broken spirit might hear an angel chorus thrum with sacred joy too deep, too broad, too stirring for words alone.

Spend Christmas with me, my love. We'll shape it together, and I will help you love the Christmas you have, not the Christmas you wish you had.

Come with me because, as I said before:

Roses are red, violets are blue.
The meaning of Christmas is, "I love you."

Every last one of you.
Forever yours,
Jesus

✳ ✳ ✳

Prayer of Confession

Dear Jesus (may I call you dear?), I confess that I have underestimated your love, or maybe I have just been dodging it. I confess that I am over-invested in the feelings I want to have at Christmastime and how to manufacture them on schedule. I expect others to make me feel certain ways and then pick fights when that doesn't work. I admit that this never works. In your mercy, forgive me for looking for love in all the wrong places. Forgive whatever is going on in my spirit that prevents me from accepting your outstretched hand. Forgive me and draw me toward you in the holy communion that is both our hearts' desire. Amen.

Questions for Reflection

1. "You are what Christmas means to me," Jesus says in this letter. He imagines himself in the pulpit preaching a one-word Christmas sermon—"You." Does this startle you, or do you find yourself nodding vigorously in agreement? How is Christmas about you? How is it not about you?

2. What rings true for you in this letter? What bothers you? Which parts of your holiday routine need an overhaul? Who needs to be involved in discussions to make the changes you'd like to implement?

3. The word "believe" is all but ubiquitous in December. It appears on everything from TV commercials and Christmas ornaments to greeting cards and outdoor banners, but to what does the word refer? What sort of belief is being encouraged? How does Jesus talk about belief in this letter? What do

      you believe? What do you want to believe? What do you have a hard time believing?

4. What's the difference between Christmas being *on* our agenda versus Christmas *setting* our agenda? How might you celebrate Christmas after Christmas? See Luke 1:46-56 to help you consider this question.

5. Where do you see the theological themes of Incarnation and Communion addressed in this letter?

Journaling Prompts

1. This letter imagines Jesus singing, "I come, for I adore you / my own precious child." What else would Jesus sing? Write out lyrics and sing them out loud.

2. Reread the selection from 1 Corinthians 13:4-8 in this letter that substituted the word "Christmas" for the word "love." Try doing the same thing with Ephesians 3:14-19, Galatians 5:23, and 2 John 1:6. Reflect on these passages in light of your plans for Christmas this year. Write and pray about what emerges for you.

3. How is Christmas directed toward children in positive ways? How does it exploit children? How have you experienced either of these in your own childhood? What experiences would you like the children in your life to have this Christmas after reading this letter? How could you use your time and resources to have a longer lasting impact on the wellbeing of children, including those other than your own?

4. Do you feel stressed? Anxious? Overscheduled? Distracted? Try the following:

Plant your feet firmly on the floor. Relax the muscles in your face. Relax the muscles in your neck and shoulders.

Inhale slowly. Pause. Exhale slowly. Pause again. Do this several times.

Ask yourself, "How do I feel?" Silently, form your response. Ask yourself, "How else do I feel?" Find the words for your feelings and name them. None are off limits. Name and release them.

Now, listen to Jesus. Read the next lines slowly out loud.

Be still and know that I am here.
Be still and know that I am love.
Be still and know that you and I are intermingled, you in me,
     I in you, love enfleshed.
Be still and know the spiritual reality of now, of you-with-me
     and me-with-you.
Be still and know Christmas.

Reread any of the lines that you would like to hear again. On a blank page of your journal, write what comes to mind after this meditation. End with "Amen," which means, "so be it."

Closing Prayer

Jesus, I am gloriously and delightfully confused as to whether Christmas is all about me or all about you. Kindle in me a sacred imagination that holds both of these truths together. Help me cast aside my reluctance, throw caution to the wind, and open the doorway of my heart to all the wonder of you, here and now. Teach me to love what you love (including myself), want what you want, and do what you would do. Help me to shape Christmas in a way that means just as much to you as it does to me—a Christmas where the mighty are toppled from their thrones, even if one of the toppled ones turns out to be me. You offer me your hand, and I accept. You offer to help me love the Christmas I have, not the Christmas I wish I had. I accept your help, and I am ready for it. Amen.

CHAPTER THIRTEEN

A Letter from You

Step 1: Don't Put This Book Down Yet

The biblical characters in this book have finished their work. They've done the best they could to put Christmas into their own words. They've signed their names, put down their pens, put away their paper, sealed their letters, and sent them off into the world.

What happens next is in your hands. With everything you've read still fresh in your mind, now is the perfect time to discern what Christmas means to you.

In this last chapter, I imagine myself sliding my pen and paper across the table to you. Here, take them. Use them to write a letter of your own. What does Christmas mean to you? Write it down, and as you write, try and match the vulnerability of the biblical characters with a vulnerability of your own.

Chances are, you'll want to skip this part. The procrastinators of the world will promise to come back to it later when there's more time. Some, who don't feel confident in their ability to put thoughts into words, may hesitate to even try. Others, who dislike writing altogether, will say they have to attend to more urgent matters. But I say, if there's even half a chance that God has been speaking to you through the letters in this book, what could be more important than taking the time to listen, linger, and think things through?

So, don't put this book down. Stay with these characters a little longer. Flip back and re-read your favorite chapters. Write out a list of your favorite lines. Think about how each letter speaks to you. What rings true? What doesn't?

Step 2: Write Your Letter

First, decide to whom you are writing. You can decide later whether you actually want to share what you've written or not, but it's a good idea to have someone in mind as you write. Picturing the person you are writing to can make it easier to put thoughts into words.

Now, set aside a block of uninterrupted time and get started. Write your letter. If you're not sure where to begin, think about the following questions:

- What does Christmas mean to you?
- What has Christmas meant to you in the past?
- What do you want Christmas to mean?
- What do you make of Christmas the way we celebrate it today?
- What could you make of it instead?
- How will you go about putting your intentions into actions?

Write until you've exhausted yourself. Write until you've emptied everything onto the page, or at least as far as you are able. Then, sign your name with a flourish.

Congratulations! You've done some original theological thinking that is authentic and true to who you are! What you've written may not be ready for public consumption but that was never the point.

Step 3: Notice Whatever Happens Next

Thinking differently *about* Christmas is one thing but acting differently *because of* Christmas is something else altogether. That's the real point. Christmas is what Christmas does.

Re-read your letter as if the only person it was meant for all along was you. Ask God to help you take your own words to heart.

Step 4: Lean into the Changes

Tuck your letter away some place special. Return to it from time to time in the days, weeks, months, or even years to come. Add a P.S. whenever any new insights come to mind.

From now on, resolve to give Christmas your full consent. Let it have its glorious way with you. Recognize it to be what it has always claimed to be: "good tidings of great joy for all the people" (Luke 2:10). Look. Listen. Remain alert. Watch for every instance where divine grace meets human longing—in yourself, in others, in communities, and in the world.

Read Colossians 3:16-17 substituting the word "Christmas" for the word "Christ." Then, do what it says:

Let the Word of [Christmas] dwell in you richly; teach and admonish one another in all wisdom; and with gratitude in your hearts sing psalms, hymns, and spiritual songs to God. And whatever you do, in word or deed, do everything in the name of the Lord Jesus, giving thanks to God the Father through him.

Eugene Peterson's paraphrase of these verses comes even closer to what I'm really trying to say:

> Let the Word of Christmas—the Message—have the run of the house. Give it plenty of room in your lives. Instruct and direct one another using good common sense. And sing, sing your hearts out to God! (Colossians 3:16-17, MSG)

I hope you have a merrier Christmas than you ever imagined, this year and in the years to come!

A NOTE FOR CLERGY
AND CHURCH LEADERS

Taking the Chance

Each year, the Advent/Christmas season offers a four-or-five-week window when people who otherwise brunch, do errands, go for a run, or sleep in on Sunday mornings persuade themselves to change their routine and go to church. Some combination of tradition, memory, and spiritual yearning strikes a sacred chord deep within. Clergy and church leaders know this. We feel something resembling desperation as we start planning for the season and find ourselves asking what we can possibly do this year that we haven't already tried. The holidays present a better than average chance for a person to meet God at the very contact point where God meets humanity—in the explosive, world-changing, life-transforming holiness of the Incarnation. We don't want to blow that chance!

The letters in this book were born out of that feeling resembling desperation. One year during Advent, I experimented with a letter-writing format for my sermons, hoping for a way to escape the tropes and clichés to which every preacher is prone. I didn't want to kill Christmas with explanations. I wanted to create Christmas moments—epiphanies—in the spaces the sermon opens up between the preacher and the person sitting in the pew. I wanted the result to be more than the sum of its parts, and I wanted to shift both the responsibility and the authority for biblical interpretation from the preacher to the listener. I wanted to bring many, many more voices to the theological table.

This book is the happy result of that experiment. It tells the truth not by purporting to recreate what happened exactly as it happened, but by presenting what can be known of the Christmas proclamation, accounting for the passage of time and changing cultural norms and contexts. Each character-driven letter speaks to that truth, but none of them speaks the whole truth. Taken together, the letters in this book comprise a lively theological conversation intended to promote a myriad of theological conversations among all whose faith (or lack of faith) drives them to seek understanding.

Using this Book in Your Context

I can imagine any number of ways to use this book in a church setting. Everything from Sunday morning adult education to mid-week study groups—either in-person or virtual—to weekly Advent dinners featuring dramatic readings and roundtable discussion would be conducive for readers to engage with the letters presented in this book.

The book might also serve as the focal point that connects the church's worship life with its educational programming. The letters could be read aloud during services in lieu of a traditional sermon. Adult and children's groups might study each Sunday's featured character in an age-appropriate format. Consider providing art supplies for children to draw the biblical characters and then find creative ways to display their art work. For a hands-on activity, children might create a simple nativity set over the course of the series that includes both the well-known and lesser-known characters featured in this book.

The prayers accompanying each letter could be used as part of your worship service and the questions for reflection could be printed in your worship bulletin or used as the basis for an informal coffee-hour discussion with the pastor immediately after worship. You might work with your church musicians to select hymns and anthems that relate to each character in addition to the standard Advent and Christmas fare. If you can't find something in your hymnal that works, write something that does!

Consider inviting church members or special guests with theatrical experience to the pulpit each Sunday to present one of the letters dramatically. The presenters might wear biblical robes from your church's costume closet or contemporary clothing that brings out the nuances of each character as he or she might be perceived today. Incorporate a prop or symbolic object into your worship center related to each character to provide additional visual resonance.

Ask members of your congregation to loan their nativity sets to the church for a display during December. Small-group leaders might do an internet search and print out images of Christian art that represent a variety of cultural and artistic visions of the stories being shared in each letter of this book. Invite a local artist to sketch each character during worship and display the sketch afterward during the coffee hour.

If your church presents an annual Christmas pageant or live nativity, consider doing a rewrite to include some of the biblical characters you've studied in this book who aren't normally featured.

I'm sure you'll have even more—and better—ideas that fit your situation once you start delving into the material and brainstorming with your colleagues in ministry!

SUGGESTIONS FOR SMALL-GROUP STUDY

The end-of-chapter material is easily adaptable for small-group study and discussion, but group leaders will need to make some up-front decisions.

Determine Scope and Frequency

Does your group want to study the whole book, one chapter per week, culminating with Advent, Christmas, and Epiphany? If yes, you'll need to start the first week of October. Another option is to double up, studying two chapters each week, beginning in mid-November. A third option would be to select certain chapters to discuss together and invite group members to read the remaining chapters on their own.

Reading or Hearing the Letters?

Decide whether your group will read the letters on their own and come together for discussion, or whether your group will listen to the letters being read dramatically each week. For the latter, be sure to line up readers well in advance and allocate sufficient time (15-20 minutes) for the readings. There are great reasons for either approach!

What's Your Angle?

Does your group enjoy straight-up Bible study? If yes, they might be interested in comparing the highlighted scriptures with the corresponding letter. Does your group enjoy quiet contemplation? Consider giving time during each meeting for centering prayer and journaling. Does your group look to one another for a time of personal sharing and support? If so, then be sure to establish a covenant of confidentiality at the beginning, select open-ended questions, and be ready to incorporate what has been shared into a closing prayer each week. In short, know what your group is looking for and clarify your role as a discussion leader and facilitator.

Preparing Your Space

Create a welcoming atmosphere with candles, colorful fabrics, prints of Christian art that feature each week's biblical character, or a nativity scene in a prominent location. Consider inviting different group members to bring a new nativity set each week.

Sample One-Hour Session

10 minutes   Welcome, Check-In with Group Members, Opening Prayer

If your nativity scene includes a figure of the character featured in the day's lesson, pass that figure around the room. If not, pass around an object that will represent that character in his or her absence.

Ask each person to respond to either of the following questions:

- One way I am like [the featured biblical character] is . . .
- One way I am not like [the featured biblical character] is . . .

Note: If you'd like to host a longer session, share a piece of music or sing a hymn related to the featured character from this session's letter.

10 minutes   Read the Selected Scriptures for the Letter

Spend time together noticing what is said *and* what isn't said. Compare what we imagine with what is actually found in the text.

20 minutes   Discussion of the Letter

Use the questions for reflection in each chapter or your own open-ended questions to facilitate a discussion about the letter or letters you've chosen for this session.

Note: For longer sessions, invite one or more participants to perform a dramatic reading of the letter for the rest of the group.

10 minutes   Quiet Time for Journaling

Invite participants to use journaling prompts in each chapter.

10 minutes   Sharing Insights and Closing Prayer

Participants should be invited to share with one another, but they should also have an option to pass. If possible, incorporate some of what has been shared into your closing prayer.

ACKNOWLEDGMENTS

THERE IS A TENDENCY to romanticize spiritual writing as a solitary activity for especially holy people to undertake in an attic or a cave alone with God and a quill pen. It's not. At least, not for me. It took a village to raise this book.

That village includes all the saints of the Bloomfield Presbyterian Church on the Green, who first heard some of the letters in this book as Sunday morning sermons and who generously granted me a sabbatical that provided time for the lion's share of the writing. That village also includes the faculty and staff from Pittsburgh Theological Seminary and my colleagues from Pittsburgh Theological Seminary's first-ever Creative Writing and Public Theology cohort. I'm especially grateful to Jimmy Cajoleas, Donna Giver-Johnston, and Mary "Shan" Overton.

No one has been more excited or more patient throughout this process than my beloved husband of thirty-five years, Carlos Monteagudo. Our son, Daniel, who was working toward a master's degree in environmental management while I worked on this book, was the inspiration for the letter from Isaiah of Jerusalem in Chapter 5. I am beyond grateful to my editor, Michael Stephens, for all those times he found himself unable to toss my proposal into the circular file, to Ben Howard for going into the weeds with me on every single chapter, and to everyone else at Upper Room Books for bringing this work out into the world.

In a very real sense, my village also includes the Bible characters themselves, with whom I've fallen in love with head over heels through this writing process. I feel I know them better than ever after doing this work. During our time together, laboring over this book, they have spoken words of grace and wisdom to me, as if they knew and loved me the way God knows and loves me. I expect that's true.